GREY ECOLOGY

I0099839

Paul Virilio
translated by Drew Burk
edited by Hubertus von Amelunxen

GREY ECOLOGY

ATROPOS PRESS

ATROPOS PRESS New York . Dresden

US: 151 First Avenue # 14, New York, N.Y. 10003
Germany: Mockritzer Str. 6, D-01219 Dresden

cover design: Jason Wagner

978-0-9819462-7-6 (Hardcover)
978-0-9827067-3-2 (Paperback)

CONTENTS

PART III : La Version Originelle

Preface

Une anthropologie de l'instant est-elle seulement concevable?
— Paul Virilio, *L'Université du désastre*, Paris 2007

In his book, *The Emigrants,* W.G. Sebald mentions archival material from the 1930s found at the British Medical Society of a person having worked in the photographic laboratory for so many years that he became poisoned by the amount of silver nitrate that he had absorbed during his professional life, to the degree that he himself had become a kind of photographic plate, his face and his hands turning blue under strong light, developing in a certain sense. Man today is exposed to an extreme photosensitivity less in the emphatic sense of seeking the light than in the claustrophobic sense of being encapsulated in a world that, as photography has shown us, has come to an end of its becoming, and exposes mankind repeatedly at the very moment of this becoming end, this finitude. Few thinkers after Walter Benjamin have seized the importance of photography as an allegory of ongoing decline the way Paul Virilio has, seizing, reflecting and mourning, committed to social action and being the *revelationary.* "The photograph," he says, "has become the most emblematic object of all we have described, more than the fastest motor," and, of course photography is at the very origin of the dromosphere. Rodolphe Toepffer stated in the early 1840s that photography, exposing us to the most distant places of the planet earth, shall lead us to abandon all notions of distance and proximity. Photography was the first 'polluter' of distance, founding in a way the *grey ecology*, which was the topic of a two-day seminar we had with Paul Virilio in La Rochelle, near the ancient harbor towers and medieval fortifications. In a way, the Collège International de Philosophie, from the times when an open controversial reflection was still desirable, moved with Paul Virilio to La Rochelle, leaving behind its shell at the rue d'Ulm in Paris.

Some fifty students from around the world took part in this seminar initiated by the European Graduate School, and for them the two days in April 2007 truly were a revelation. This volume consisting of the transcription and translation of the seminar as well as a series of responding articles by scholars, bears testimony not only to the extraordinary vividness of Paul Virilio's engagement as urbanist, as thinker and as teacher, but also to the realm his thinking inhabits in the world today. His book on the University of Disaster has since been published, seeking a university where Arts and Sciences meet to think about the accidents of substances and the accidents of knowledge, where the finitude of the becoming will guide a thinking that considers the world after the world within the world. We are in definite need of this university, and I think we had in fact entered into it in those days in April in La Rochelle.

I would like to thank especially Drew Burk for his dedication to this volume, for the hard work of transcribing and the rewarding and diligent translation of the seminar, the EGS students for their well-prepared and engaged participation, the other contributors to this volume for their critical responses to the seminar. And beyond the seminar, my thanks also to Wolfgang Schirmacher for his dedication to the most singular and challenging School: the EGS, to the University of La Rochelle and the Centre Intermondes for their warm hospitality, and to Paul Virilio for his dramatic and breathtaking optimism as an urbanist un-building the fortresses of globally calculated convictions of eternal accidents.

Hubertus von Amelunxen, March 2009

Translator's Acknowledgements

This translation is derived from a transcription of copious hours of dialogue between Paul Virilio and his students, his public during the two-day seminar in La Rochelle where he shared with us many themes of his life's work. Even for Virilio, to express one's work over a 10 hour period is akin to a test of endurance and demands an almost super-human effort. As the transcriber and translator of this discussion, I have tried to maintain not only a closeness to his ideas, which he would say can never be anything but an approximation, but also perhaps more importantly his performative agency, his vocal rhythm. I hope that at least a hint of this Virilian rhythm emerges in the following discourse. I would first like to thank Paul Virilio for his complicity in this work. I would also like to thank Hubertus von Amelunxen, Wolfgang Schirmacher and Sylvère Lotringer for their suggestions and amicable support in this daunting venture. My thanks also go not only to the EGS students and alumni for their vital questions, but to Virginia Cutrufelli, Christine Marx, Henri de Serrey, Jean-Christophe Plantin, John David Ebert, Amelie Morgan and Jason Wagner for their suggestions in the editing process of both the transcription and translation.

Translator's Introduction
The Man of the Crowd
Drew Burk

From a generation of painters, an architect of disappearance surfaces. A man of the crowd, Virilio was always very close to those who hoped to stare down the militarization of existence, and in doing so, to allow for a strategic creative perception of an artist who realized abstract art, while mimicking the death of concrete meaning, was not just an opening to the subconscious, but to how our perception was changing due to the trauma of war, or existence. For, while he has been considered a harsh critic of art, like any artist worth his salt, Virilio was never concerned with the definition of art, but how it related to reality as such. The futurists and their call for an all-out war, a pure war against existence, is telling for Virilio. He is not against art, but as a "child of the blitzkrieg," he understood Marinetti perhaps better than Marinetti. War is hell. And so when art comes around to parody this hell, Virilio knows that art shifts its position. Art shifts from the parody of reality to the uncanny position of reality parodying art. Here, against this televisual carnival of screens upon screens, art lost its way. But while Virilio is chastised for his cynicism towards art, like Baudrillard, they weren't the ones to put art on trial; art had done that to itself a hundred years before. And now art has signed the deal with the digital. For Virilio it's not about what art is, but what it does. And here in the commodified world of the digital, art shifts completely. Against the backdrop of the instantaneous, the visual spectrum, the one crucial element that all art relies upon has been re-wired: no longer kinetic energy but cinematic energy. Once the WWII bombardier, with his radar and coordinates, no longer saw an enemy, but a target on a screen, the disembodiment was already digging its way into the telematic spectrum that is our real-time perception.

But war surely isn't the same thing today. We have embedded reporters; we have U.N. resolutions. We have presidents with YouTube publicities. If Virilio sounds like a sore loser, one of the last French cynics, it's because he is. It is his weakness that is his strength, he would say. Amidst the pundits and ventriloquists in the political media and the art world, the same sanctioned yes-men and yes-women prepare to make art/speeches with their fingers poised at the ready with jeopardy-like buzzer responses, Virilio takes pause, knowing better than anyone that progress comes with failure.

While we have moved from the atomic bomb to the information bomb and on to the genetic bomb, we are witnessing a destruction of a different nature. Technology is not the end for Virilio. He is not developing a thesis *against* the televisual field in politics or art. He does the dirty work. As an architect, he recognizes our current real-time position not merely as the technological site of disaster, but more importantly as a site of the accident. For this is how reality functions today and perhaps since the beginning: accident upon accident. Only now, with the dromologic nature of existence, the accident happens before we know it has happened. Causes appear to come after the effects, and this is where art and technology must take into consideration their own destructive mechanics, not that they shouldn't be transgressive, but in assuming a role of continuous sped up transgression, motives and intentions are no longer predictable even to the artist, scientist, or spectator. In the realm of real-time, reaction time becomes paralyzed.

But Virilio is not a pessimist. He is not decrying the end of art, or the end of philosophy, or transgressive thought. On the contrary, he is, as an architect, providing a guide for living instantaneity. And this is where his work on *grey ecology* is of the utmost importance; his work is not that of the "ready-made" answers of the New Philosophers or positivists. His thought is predicated on the problematic of scientific relativity itself, namely the *speed* of perception today. When one deals with speed one deals with the relationship between phenomena, and here "no mastery can be had." This is Virilio's *grey ecology*. It is a position of openness within a technological culture where operative science is seemingly closing the gap on the question mark and leaving only room for the period.

Virilio's position against a "technology of progress" is quite well known, but what would technology say to Virilio? How would the technical or a "technology of 'progress'" classify Virilio? For while he looks at it, hallucinates about it, does technology hallucinate Virilio? Paul Virilio has taken on many nametags such as philosopher, urbanist, architect, essayist. These (*our/are*) his names. Those who have made Paul Virilio known, the crowd, or audience to which Virilio speaks is perhaps not the one that speaks to *him*...most of the time. Virilio, in placing himself and his work within what he calls the *espace critique*, the critical space itself, namely in the space between, in the space where the physics of relativity begins to show itself, is taking on a position of delirium.

Virilio, citizen of the atomic age, experiencing the hallucinatory delirium of the void, always hovers around the position between destruction and creation, between the subject and the object. This is precisely the state of the pure subject of the crowd. Virilio's public is where we were heading. Some would say Virilio speaks a bizarre, excessive, Catholic, or even defensive response to the age of the hyperreal and the digital. Virilio makes no bones about his position as a Christian. But rarely does he become a lobbyist for Christianity, if only to mention the inspirational madness of Bob Dylan or Jimi Hendrix. Virilio, like a mother wanting to make sure her children look both ways before crossing the street, is aware of the fragility of existence. It is his asthmatic reaction to his apocalyptic revealing.

And it is indeed Virilio's use of this word apocalypse, that makes him a target for criticism from those who maintain that his writings are of an outmoded ethos. But his detractors who don't take the time to listen are not his public either. When Virilio states his position is that of an apocalyptic thinker, it is in the sense of a revelatory thinker. Apocalypse signifies revelation for Virilio. This is his main position: as a revealer of the delirium of the crowd (à la Poe). Virilio's thought, with its main focus on dromology, the study of speed, and for him thus technology and war, suggests the obvious here: one must not speak to a public as such, one must speak to the crowd yet to come who is already here. What does this mean? His public is every one of us: those who press the visual flesh against the technical screen-world of instantaneity. Virilio's thought takes the position of a phenomenological revealing. But his claim of being more an essayist than a philosopher is of a different vein. Virilio's phenomenology, his dromology, is one that has no "answers" proper. It is not concerned with the concrete thought of the New Philosophers, with the "ping-pong", theoretical kangaroo boxing matches of the tele-born. In the real-time age where answers are arrived at before the questions themselves are posed, we are no longer in need of artists of the rational as such. Once we have entered into the realm of real-time, of the instantaneity of perception, in the realm of the tele-born, the standardization of the medium, what Virilio calls "tele-optics," becomes predicated on a mode of thought that does not lend itself to a concrete philosophy or a precise "rational" thought at all. And this is where Virilio's position as a phenomenological revealer begins to take shape. From his vantage point as architect, Virilio understands the need to re-evaluate the progress of our technological position. And here, the artist can only find his/her place within the trajectory of technology by taking into consideration their own bodily position to tele-optics and stereo-optics. In the realm of dromology there is no possible position of understanding; one can only maintain a relational position between phenomena. Here, the subjective position takes on the schizo-subject of the hyper-speed realm of technology. Here, no answers are possible, here, as Virilio states, "all one can do is guess." But Virilio's position is not one of pure guessery. His extrapolationist position against his delirium state exhibits the architecture of a 23rd century scientist: three-parts fractal geometry, two-parts theory of general relativity, one-part Philip K. Dick.

Elegy for a dead friend

I must say that before meeting and interpreting for Virilio, I
had quite a few problems with his writings, especially
concerning art. I was more akin to his friend and theoretical
antagonist, Jean Baudrillard, and while I desperately wanted to
enjoy both of these thinkers' philosophical inquiries into the
mediated world that we find ourselves immersed in today,
Virilio's thought, as opposed to Baudrillard's, at the least
seemed too defensive. But as Virilio began to plead his case,
his presence gave another quality to his work. I couldn't help
but deconstruct the scene. Virilio, in the aftermath of his
friend's death (Baudrillard had died two weeks prior) seemed
more concerned than ever with maintaining a "distance" from
what Baudrillard would name the hyperreal. Virilio's critique
of the Deleuzian "society of control" is one we all can
understand at a certain level. Speed and technology carry with
it the accident. "With an 800-seat passenger jet, 800 deaths..."
It is not difficult to understand the dichotomy of what Virilio
calls the successful failure...the accident of progress... But
something struck me quite curiously here when Virilio
proposed his grey ecology and with it a *recoil*, a necessity to
take a step back from the instantaneity of what he calls
"cinematic energy" in order to maintain a distance. One
started to see a certain difference in the unfolding of Virilio's
critique and that of his friend Jean Baudrillard. As Virilio
described the serious problematic that technological progress
poses with regard to perception and the process of becoming
"tele-optically correct," as he spoke of a public to come who
must deal with the tele-optic glaucoma of having "blinders"
on, he seemed to rely on a novel type of distance, where one
would study the accident, this progress, this disaster of
technology. Virilio would call this position of study the
University of Disaster.

Virilio, who called himself "a child of the blitzkrieg," was
someone who, at first, I thought perhaps was trying to evoke
the end. But throughout the entire conference, his constant re-
affirmation, of proportions, forms, and finitude as opposed to
the end showed me something different. It is impossible not to

see the Christian ether surrounding Virilio. When he responded to a question regarding what artists today should do to fight the problem of speed and technology, he quoted St. Augustine, "Do whatever you want, but do it with love." But for Virilio there is an interesting twist that makes all the difference. His idea of revelation is not that of the end, but of a revealing, and this for Virilio is the essence as well of his concept of the integral accident.

This leads me to Baudrillard and his relationship to Virilio. Virilio believes the biogenetic bomb is one we must be wary of. He warns against cloning not only of people, but of perception itself. Virilio however does not believe that we have already entered the "hyperreal" of Baudrillard. I asked him the question. He thinks we have yet to move over. Virilio still claims we can gain the necessary distance from the technological speed of the virtual. But Baudrillard obviously thought differently. He states, "Distance is obliterated, both external distance from the real world and the internal distance specific to the sign" (*The Intelligence of Evil or the Lucidity Pact*).

Virilio calls for us to take a step back from the instantaneity of screen technology, but for Baudrillard, it has already burned itself onto our retina. For Baudrillard, the cloning that Virilio speaks of has already taken place, perhaps not physically yet, (this is debatable, but at least psychically with the mass popularization of certain figures, styles, etc.). For Baudrillard, the hyperreal has already taken over, and more to the point, we have entered the realm of the pataphysical, the theatre of cruelty that is the science of imaginary solutions. The "integral accident" of Virilio is as always/already framed in the theatre of the global. But Baudrillard reminds us of the place to which thought should not be instructed, to an idea which he and his friend Virilio would perhaps have agreed upon. Baudrillard states, "Thought must refrain from instructing or being instructed by, a future reality, for, in that game, it will always fall into the trap of a system that holds the monopoly of reality. And this is not a philosophical choice. It is, for thought, a life-and-death question." (*Ibid*)

And this brings me to a point on which I think both of these philosophers (one always reminding us of his architectural hauntology, the other of his Jarry nature) can agree. They are both trying to carve out a thought and a mimetic mirror of actuality without coming to a limit, an absolute. When Virilio quotes St. Augustine, it is in the same way that Baudrillard makes up a fake quote from Ecclesiastes (See: *Simulacres et Simulations*). It is for a love of existence, even if it is the smallest of things.

Works Cited

J. Baudrillard, *The Intelligence of Evil or The Lucidity Pact* trans. Chris Turner (New York: Berg, 2005)

J. Baudrillard, *Simulacres et Simulation* (Paris: Galilee, 1981)

P. Virilio, *Art and Fear* trans. Julie Rose (London: Continuum, 2003)

P. Virilio, *The Information Bomb* (London: Verso, 2000)

P. Virilio, *Open Sky* trans. Julie Rose (London: Verso, 1997)

P. Virilio, *Ville Panique* (Paris: Galilée, 2005)

PART I: Grey Ecology

Session I
Introduction to Grey Ecology

What are we waiting for when we no longer need to wait in order to arrive? We are waiting for the arrival of what remains. — Paul Virilio

I am an urbanist and philosopher. It's not out of modesty that I say this, but because philosophy was born in the city. I am an urbanist, but perhaps essayist, as opposed to philosopher, is the best definition for what I am. I am also claustrophobic, and you will understand why after this discussion.

At this moment, there is much being said about green ecology, that is to say, about the draining of our resources and global warming. This lecture that I present to you is approximate. Dromology and the dromosphere, the acceleration of reality and not merely of history, is an approximation. In my opinion, there can never be an absolute response to this. Why? Dromology is at the heart of relativity itself. I remind you that speed is not a phenomenon. It is a relation between phenomena. It is relativity itself. And from the moment we find ourselves confronted with mathematics, from the moment we find ourselves in front of this mathematical language, in my opinion, we cannot lay claim to precision regarding dromology.

A professor at Valence recently completed a thesis attempting to illustrate the approximate dimension of my work. It is not out of modesty, approximation for me, in the area of speed, is a capital phenomenon. There is no precision when it comes to speed. (There is a phenomenon between time and space.) Thus, dromology is not a closed, complete theory. It is obvious, speed and accident are linked and it is from here that we get the idea of an approximation. It is certainly a discipline which is open and offered up to other interpretations, and it is from this openness that we find the link with ecology, green ecology—ecology linked to nature and grey ecology, which opens itself up to the cosmos, to culture. Here no mastery is possible.

If there were a professor who wrote a treatise on dromology, I don't think I would read it, not out of pride of being the author, but because it wouldn't interest me. Why? Because relativity leads us to study two orders of magnitude, the magnitude of distance and of science, and the mathematical disciplines and the magnitude of poverty, the magnitude of weakness; these two orders are linked. It is from this that one sees an interest in finitude. Those who look at the work done on grey ecology often analyze my contribution to it as an apocalyptic work. This is not true. Dromology is not the "end of the world." I often say that the concept "end of the world" is a concept without a future. No, what interests me is the "finitude of the world." It is claustrophobia. What is the "finitude of the world?" It is that an apple is only an apple, a man is only a man, and a world is only a world. That is the "finitude of the world."

So, my interest here today, via the dromosphere, is the passage and the acceleration of history and the acceleration of reality through new technologies, it is the foreclosure of the world. It is the closing-in of the world. The pollution of time and distance is much more severe, in my opinion, than the pollution of material substances. The self-created world coinciding with the natural world also causes its own pollution. With the pollution of nature, there is green ecology. Grey ecology is the pollution of the self-created world. I bring to your attention again that I am more an architect than a philosopher, and somewhere the history of the size of proportions, of dimensions is important to me. Vastness, size or proper dimensions are elements that are not really taken into consideration regarding phenomena. I remind you, a little digression here, that I published three books, one in 1976, *L'insecurité du territoire*, which already prefaced the twilight of place. In 1984, paying homage to George Orwell, I published, *L'espace critique*, and in 1990, *L'inertie polare,* the first book which speaks of the twilight of place. From this you can understand the essential introduction for me today of the temporal contraction of the inhabited communal geosphere. What one calls in computer science, a temporal convection.

I repeat that the temporal contraction reduces almost to nothing the vast reach of the globe, of the habitable geosphere of the common world. There is only one world: the dromosphere. Somewhere the dromosphere reduces to nothing the geosphere, or if you like, the biosphere. Real-time, the instantaneity of tele-communications and the creation of the internet are an earthquake of time for biodiversity and geodiversity. When we speak of pollution, we speak often of material pollution. This is quite false. It is the urbanist and the architect who say this, that there is pollution of distances and of the scale of the world (*la grandeur nature*). There is no grandeur without dimensions. There is no object without proportions. There is no man without dimensions. It is finally materialism, I think we can use the term here, without forgetting the notion of scales of size, the notion of scales and proportions of things in space and time from different substances. It is surprising how easily we link nature to culture, yet we easily forget size. This is the question I evoke in my book *L'Espace critique (Critical Space)* which gives its name to my collection and which published Baudrillard, and Guattari. "Critical Space" is not only a time, the instant, but it is also a space. The architect, that I am, puts into action all of his material construction in first constructing the proportions that give that measurement of the building. This is crucial. He constructs the proportions before constructing concrete or stone. What we call real-time leads to the space-time continuum suffering a temporal contraction which reduces to nothing or practically nothing the vastness of the world. This doesn't do damage in the same way that global warming and water depletion does. Alas, it is of a different gravity. Real-time is an earthquake of time. Great or weak, this vastness constitutes the power of Being. And now I'll give you a very clear example: to be a man is to measure basically between one and two meters, at the maximum, between a dwarf and a giant. If a man measures 20 meters in height, it is not a man. This is unthinkable. Today, everything is like this. It is amazing to what degree proportions have disappeared from the modern world. This is where I get the two orders of magnitude that I spoke of earlier which are equivalent. One is the weak half of the other. There are two orders of magnitude: the magnitude of power; one speaks in particular of the power of the United States, this is a reality; but the magnitude of poverty is also a reality of the same order. And here, the terms of measurement and of excess address themselves to restoration. In grey ecology, the terms of measurement and excess also refer to restoration, to the retention of the vastness of the world. In grey ecology the terms of measurement and excess (*démesure*) do not refer to the "hyper" – *the outside* of astrophysics, but to the restriction and retention of the vastness of the world.

From the 20th century to the present, we are heading today and tomorrow towards a lamentation point where man's impotence explodes. In fact, the excessive character of the contraction of the ecology in transportation and the excessive character of the acceleration of the reality of the world and its continuum, not only conditions nature and our trajectories and movements, but culture and history as well.

Or, to put it another way, history contracts at the same time as its geography. Here again, I am an urbanist, and I can tell you that history and the city are linked to a contraction: to the concentration of globalization, and of the successful failures of techno-science. It is the failure of a success and not a failure due to error. This contraction, of the acceleration of reality, is the failure of the successes of the operating sciences of progress. I argue, particularly in a book I am writing and which will be called the *Université du desastre (The University of Disaster)*, I argue science will suffer an accident due to the finitude of the world, that is to say, due to the spatial-temporal contraction which has conditioned the places of Being and things. The temporal contraction does not simply concern transportation and live telephoning on the internet. What is it then that we're dealing with? It concerns knowledge. The retention of the space-time of the world concerns primarily science and philosophy. It is from here that we see the idea in the work of Aristotle, the idea of speaking about the accident of substances. There is going to be, there already has been, an accident of ideas. Ideas are linked to the vastness and the measurement of the world. All of our sciences are linked to the geography of the world. They are not simply linked to the history of knowledge, but also to the expanse that follows its own knowledge. And this is why we need the University of Disaster.

I want to talk about fear and about the claustrophobia I mentioned earlier. The fear of acceleration is not yet here, but certain people, who are claustrophobic, or asthmatic, already feel this fear: the fear of exhausting the geo-diversity of the world. I will give you an example. I have been to Venice twice. It is an extraordinary city. I had a friend who showed me this and that part of town. Finally he said we should go see several more places and then I would have seen everything. I said no. I wanted to keep Venice unknown, so I would be able to come back and visit. For some reason, I didn't want to exhaust Venice. I did not want to participate in the twilight of places.

For example, the capability of experiencing the antipodes (North and South Pole) as a tourist, fatally restrains the expanse of the geophysical power of the world. Besides this sacred world, no other world is inhabitable at the moment. And this fear, this anxiety, the claustrophobia that infects certain adults, will soon become a phenomenon of the masses. This is the fear behind the great ecological imprisonment about which Foucault spoke regarding the asylum and a carceral universe. Imagine tomorrow that this feeling of grand imprisonment no longer concerns merely the placing into prison of one individual or another, but the grand imprisonment of a world too small for its inhabitants. This is anxiety. Imagine in one or two generations, at the end of the week, going to the circus in Tokyo, heading to New York for drinks, and the next day, heading back to work, and all that for a dollar or two. *Open Sky*, it's less and less expensive, imagine this universe where things will already be there, already viewed, already given. In France, tourism no longer only concerns the few, it is localized, it externalizes them, is beyond them. There are many experiencing this situation: young, rich, old, and poor, until it becomes a mass phenomenon. It will become a cosmopolitical (*cosmo-politique*) phenomenon.

This worry is already present. Are you aware of the research done by certain astrophysicists who deal with exo-planets, and the problematic of the great externalization from one day to the next? Let me cite a claim of the great British astrophysicist, Stephen Hawking. "When we have decided to set our sights on other planets, our future will be assured." Another way of putting it: our future depends on planets which are uninhabitable. Within the solar system as we know it, he says, we would need 50 thousand years to discover an inhabitable one. With new technologies and new research, we could perhaps render this exploit possible, but the voyage would take at least 6 years. When a man like Hawking, a scientist, states a phrase like this, that is to say, that the future of humanity depends on the colonization of another world which doesn't exist, without water, without air, the question is already there, this anxiety, this claustrophobia. He has this worry because it is precisely what he is working on. Have you read the research on exo-planets? Here the other day, at the Aquarium of La Rochelle, there was a test concerning exo-oceans. What is an exo-ocean? It is an exotic ocean. Maybe on Europa, the moon of the planet Jupiter, there might be an ocean under ice. There might be an ocean. As one astronomer from NASA stated, "that ocean has too much water, ok, it is how many light years away from here?" You see the expanse? Another way to understand this anxiety of humanity to which I am speaking is to think of the process of an asthma attack. It is this same anxiety that is induced when dealing with survival.

I like to work, you know, on spaces of enclosure. When one hears the declaration by Stephen Hawking that I just cited, "When we have set our sights on other planets, our future shall be assured," it means that the astrophysicist is the substitute for the geophysicist. For me, this is a delirium. It is the delirium of a science deprived of a philosophical conscience, of the failure of success: the failure of the success of progress. The failure of progress is the failure of progress' success up against the finitude of the world. It is the failure of progress' spectacular achievement. I am not against progress. I am saying that it is wonderfully catastrophic. The failure of the spectacular achievement is found in all areas: anthropology, energy and information regarding matter. It is found in all areas but one: the wisdom of the discernment of the end, the discerning of finitude. This spectacular achievement of the exact sciences, of operational science and not only for knowledge, has not taken into account the end, death. It has not taken into account finitude and the fact that the world is only a world and science is only a limited science. As the saying goes, "scientific truth is an error living on borrowed time."

This is why I cannot work on speed without working on the accident. Speed and the accident are linked. Here, what I just described is what I call the "Integral Accident." Until now, scientific accidents, techno-scientific accidents as opposed to natural accidents like an earthquake, were local accidents. For example, a bomb explodes *somewhere*. The pollution of a fire was *somewhere*, etc. Today, the accident becomes integral. It affects the expanse of the common world. We are replacing the expanse of the world with speed. This is truly an integral accident. The replacing of the expanse of the world with speed, with the speed of transportation, or electromagnetic transmission, cannot be done without provoking a serial accident which concerns both the effects of kinetic energy and what I call the cinematic energies of the acceleration of reality. And this leads us to fatally disrupt history and geography: the great enclosure of the 21st century goes way beyond the incarceration of the 18th century and the era of the Panopticon denounced by Foucault, after having been announced by Jeremy Bentham. It is this 21st century enclosure that is the big question today. What? Real-time, it's going "live." It's the tele-objectivity of the world. It's Google-Earth. We have gone from megalomania to megalopsychia.

The approach I take is the study of the dromosphere and of the acceleration of reality. Real-time is still in the real space of geography. The fear of the great enclosure has a name. It is what the elders of the siege called "obsidian fever." I remind you that I have worked quite a bit on the strategies linked to war, sieges, etc. I will give you an extraordinary example of "obsidian fever": the Warsaw ghetto. There is a great journalist who spoke to me about the Warsaw Ghetto, I forget his name, I can't give you the reference, but there was one thing I have never forgotten. It was in the middle of winter and the journalist noticed it stank of coal and that all the windows were open. He asked people why they left their windows open in the middle of winter, and they said, "We are already under siege, you don't want us to close the window as well?" This is "obsidian fever." Except, here, the "obsidian fever" is that of a city or a ghetto. Imagine it tomorrow, a state of urgency on a world scale from a new technology, which is itself a siege of the world. A state of deception: that of the progress of reality, the progress of transportation, the origin of the radio, the origin of telecommunications, of microchips with radio-frequencies. A state of deception, a state of urgency, a state of siege, suppressing our public liberty, only there is no tyrant behind it all, suppressing them. They are suppressed by the enclosure of the world, the foreclosure of the world. There is no longer a need for a tyrant. Be assured, I am not in despair. I believe it is time to open the University of Disaster. Winston Churchill once remarked, "An optimist sees an opportunity behind every calamity."

Question: This reminds me of Platonic measure.

Paul Virilio: I am a relativist. No, I only think that one can't be an architect, an urbanist, that is to say, a man of proportions, in denying measure. It is not a matter of moral measure, to maintain the order of things. That is geophysics. When you see someone you are attracted to, you say that they have "nice proportions." This is not a moral question. Having said this, it is true, that the root is there. Between the Egyptians and the Greeks, we had the question of measure. No, I think that we have forgotten this understanding, that if a man measures 1 meter 60 or 2 meters, he is a man and that if he measures 20 meters, he is no longer a man. It is so ridiculous to say that, but one could say that it hasn't been passed on to our culture. And it's curious; there is also this denial of the small. There is grandeur (magnitude) in the grains of wheat, an incommensurability. The magnitude of the atom, the magnitude of a grain of wheat. There is a sort of disqualification of everything that is small, a magnitude of smallness and not a magnitude of the small. There is something else that heads in the same direction as the denial of the magnitude of poverty for the benefit of that of wealth in the economic order. Here it is spatial economy: proportions and geometry, not the other economy, the economy of goods. From the spatial economy we get the reference to the magnitude of poverty. It was Jacques-Bénigne Bossuet who spoke of the importance of the two magnitudes, which are inseparable: the magnitude of poverty and the magnitude of power. We are in the middle of forgetting the magnitude of poverty, but ecology is going to bring us back to this order whether it is through a grey or green ecology.

Question: You speak about us forgetting the magnitude of the small, of proportions, but is this a forgetting or a sort of shortcut to which we have become addicted?

Paul Virilio: It is not a question of forgetting, but of colonization. Colonization is a phenomenon that overrides colonial politics. It conquers, it exploits, and it gets out of there. I think it was Pétain who said, a large colony means a large navy. It is technology that promotes the colony. The navy of today is aeronautics: the spaceships that go to other planets. We can't speak of colonization without speaking of the maritime power and the grandeur of the aerial power becoming astronautic. Thus, somewhere, colonial ideology is part of operative science. It conquers, it discovers something extraordinary, it exploits it, and then it leaves. Science is colonial, that is to say, operative science is not pure knowledge. Operative science is colonial.

Question: Would you speak about borders. Isn't it necessary to transgress borders? To forget proportions? Do we always have to be mindful of these proportions, and if this is the case, then don't we become defined by them? Are we defined by proportions?

Paul Virilio: I believe that we can't understand this question without saying obviously, yes. Obviously we are defined by proportions, but these proportions are not borders, they are limits. That's why the notion of limits is much more important than borders. It's for this reason that I say that the border that interests us today is the negative horizon. It is the spherical. It's not by chance that celestial objects have a spherical shape. Where is this negative border? It is the limit or negative horizon.

Question: Are proportions a limit?

Paul Virilio: Proportions are the limit of being.

Question: But proportions are relations?

Paul Virilio: Of course, and so it is with relativity and space-time. Speed is not a phenomenon; it is the relation between phenomena. That is to say, there exists a relation of spatial proportions, Euclidean geometry, and there are also temporal relations, that of relativity and the phenomenon of acceleration. One can feel to what degree the acceleration of reality disrupts everything including political phenomena, democratic phenomena. The acceleration of history, the acceleration of reality, that is to say, instantaneity, is the attribute of the divine. A man who has at his disposal the immediacy, the ubiquity of the instant, is the one who can cause a media coup. Like what Berlusconi did. It's to place oneself in a non-democratic position.

Question: Dealing with proportions through disaster, at least for me, throughout history, we have only dealt with proportions through disasters, whether it was a natural disaster or a man-made disaster. This doesn't seem to work anymore. We have transcended that and now we need technology to create disasters. How I read your book was that technology would create disasters and that this was the only way to bring back proportions. Is this what your book Strategies of Deception *is all about?*

Paul Virilio: Next to the university, there is the arsenal. The arsenal is the academy of disaster: The arsenal of Venice, all the way to the arsenal at Cherbourg. We forget that the museum of the accident, the great observatory of catastrophe, the academy of disaster has existed since the arsenal of Venice. In the operative sciences, we have invented catastrophes all the way to the atomic bomb. Or, to put it another way, this intelligence of the end is already a military intelligence. Only we need to rip this intelligence away from war, to deal with disasters. Whether it is a disaster from the military-industrial complex or a disaster of finitude which I spoke of earlier, linked to the means of transportation, and transmission.

Einstein said there were three bombs: the atomic bomb, the information bomb, and the mass genetic bomb. L'Abbé Pierre met with Einstein. They chatted, and Einstein talked about these three bombs: The atomic bomb, everyone knows what that is; the information bomb, if there is no information, the world does not exist; and the demographic bomb. One can't think of the demographic bomb without thinking of the genetic bomb. That is to say, who has the right to biotechnology?

I obviously believe that the University of Disaster is positive. It is able to confront head on this catastrophe of the finitude of progress. Considering all other means, there is no alternative in dealing with the end of progress. It is not that progress fails. It is that, in succeeding, it fails in its finitude. Speaking about telesurveillance, I am just going to relate a little anecdote. At the time of the invention of the English railroad, a humorist who was also a railroad engineer stated that the big problem with the undertaking of the railroad tracks was that it worked in both directions. So it is with telesurveillance as well.

Question: Isn't the arsenal a location for the death-drive?

Paul Virilio: Yes, it is an example, but we also have a big problem today with the kamikaze. Somewhere, the kamikaze is a leak from the arsenal. Suicide goes from an individual phenomenon to a collective phenomenon. That is to say, suicide, according to Lacan, is psychological and has now become sociological. And the extraordinary multiplication of kamikazes at this moment, is not the kamikaze, it is the multiplication of suicidal excess. When one thinks that this term comes from Japan, one must not forget that there was a kamikaze contamination in the Middle-East, moreover it was introduced by a Japanese woman, Fusaka Shigenobu, who had a liaison with a Palestinian leader. She transplanted the Japanese kamikaze which was part of her culture. Are we going to have the same problem in our culture? This is the big question. An active suicide and no longer a passive suicide. In this case, "I can't go on any longer" becomes "I can't go on any longer and I am going to blow up everything and everyone else with me."

Comment: Yes, but I think there is something different between the two types of suicide. For the kamikaze, there is a cultural origin. Whereas for the Muslims (suicide bombers), there is something much more relativistic about it.

Paul Virilio: I am quite interested in what took place before the atomic bomb. There was a very important moment in the Japanese empire. At a given moment, they envisioned a national suicide. The first sign of a national suicide was that the entire Japanese fleet, after Hiroshima, after Nagasaki, went to kill itself. At this moment, there was a question from a soldier who had a reaction and who said, "We, we can kill ourselves, that's ok, but if the army commits suicide where are we heading?" There were many debates. This reflection was fortunate, because they were tempted to move from an individual suicidal state, to a mass sociological suicide, to a national suicide. The arsenal is here with the third intelligence. H.G. Wells said that there were three types of intelligence: animal intelligence, human intelligence, and military intelligence. The atomic bomb is linked with suicide.

Session II
The Temporal Contraction

Today, like the labor pains of birth, the temporal contraction
of our daily activities and movements provokes a contraction
of distance and delay that is less a sign of a positive
advancement than that of a new type of accidental catastrophic
ecological transfer. This transfer nonetheless leaves no trace
because of the supersonic speed of aerial transports or the
instantaneity of telecommunications is always perceived as
incontestable progress. This forces us nonetheless to question
ourselves about the serious gap within an ecological science
that doesn't seem to take into account any counter-force to this
acceleration which in the end reduces to nothing the depth of
the field of our environment. The pollution of distance comes
to associate itself with the pollution of substances which is
more concerned with the expanse of the common world than
with the nature of elements. We must respect the spaces of our
daily activities, to in a way save the biodiversity of those
species on the way toward extinction. We are up against this
relativistic event which affects not only the materiality of the
human milieu, but also its space-time continuum. This event
poses itself after the question of the acceleration of history and
the acceleration of reality. With the explosion of the
cybernetic interactivity of a real-time which, from now on,
conditions the political economy of our developed societies all
the way to the weakest economies of the world, the terrestrial
star has a certain number of astronomers searching in the
universe for several exotic exo-planets with which to
substitute the planet of our narrow origins. Where will we be
if the society of consumption has spread to all nations? Not
only would our old earth not survive, but we would need at
least three more to satisfy our needs. This is where we get the
singular quest of the telluric planet for a planet three times as
vast as our own. Thus, we claim that the earthquake of
progress with the telluric contraction of distances and time is a
precursor to a birth both hoped for and dreaded, for fear of an
abnormality. There is a fear of a major handicap which would
result from this contraction of time of the biosphere for a

humanity now born of its own humus much more than from those far-off stars of which the astrophysicists speak so often. Human comes from the word humus. Humus speaks of humility.

The lyrical illusion of a growing progress leads to the conjoined apparition of nanotechnologies of the infinitely small as well as the miniaturization of the infinitely big including the only known inhabitable planet in the solar system. After the announcement at the end of the last century of the "end of history", by Francis Fukyama, we are not talking about announcing the end of geography, we are merely trying to evoke the telescoping, the accident of a time that is "real" but which does not take into account the spherical limits of the real space of a small planet in provisory suspension for cosmic life.

Question: Does this discourse put you in the camp of de-growth?

Paul Virilio: Yes, certainly, except I take de-growth to mean here deceleration.

Once again, I am not talking about de-growth at the level of consumption but at the level of deceleration. Earlier, I spoke about the austerity of the state concerning ecology. I think that there will not be de-growth without a deceleration. That is to say, we are not aware of the phenomenon of the production of speed in transportation, and transmission, etc. and they are at the heart of growth and de-growth.

Questioner's Reply: Yes, I was speaking about the thesis of economic growth.

Paul Virilio: For a long time I have said I am not an economist. Next to the economy of political wealth, we cannot afford not to make a place for a political economy of speed. Speed and wealth are tied together. Accumulation and acceleration are tied together. It is from here that we get a new intelligence of the political economy. I remind you it was the physiocrats who were the innovators of the political economy. Now, ecologists take their turn at being physiocrats in their own way when they posed the question of the political economy of speed. I believe the political economy of speed is also at the heart of the energy problem we are dealing with right now (i.e. the exhausting of our fossil fuels, etc., the nuclear problem). I say this because, if we continue to underline that nuclear power would be ideal because it doesn't pollute, and that we can have as much as we want while oil and coal are diminishing, if we continue like this in the name of ecology, we are going to basically install nuclear power everywhere. So, we see to what extent energy politics cannot exist today without an economic energy politics of the speed of all speeds. Well, this might be part of de-growth, but I am talking about deceleration. Once again, it is via the order of the relativity of time that I state that the ecological question does not simply concern the materialism of the goods of capitalism, etc.

In 1977, when I published *Vitesse et Politique (Speed and Politics)*, on the back cover there was a phrase which today has become self-explanatory. "La vitesse est la viellesse du monde." "Speed is the aging of the world." This is capital! "Speed is the aging of the world." If we take this sentence seriously, we're talking about a contraction. I am 75 years old. I tell you this because I am not as energetic as I used to be. Somewhere along the way, speed has aged me. The speed of life, because life is speed. I am energetic or less energetic. Life and speed are one and the same. So, somewhere we have to understand that we are aging the world by the phenomena of the acceleration of reality: hence my speaking of a political economy of speed.

Wolfgang Schirmacher: You speak about the speed of the exterior world, but can't we also have an interior life that becomes more and more rigorous due to the wisdom attained through experience? Rilke speaks of an interior faith.

Paul Virilio: There is quite a bit to say here. It is not easy. Personally, I don't make much of a distinction between the exterior and interior. Contrary to my old friend Jean Baudrillard, I have no psychoanalytic culture; zero, it doesn't interest me. This being said, I am quite aware that this accident of reality, the acceleration of reality and not that of history is an unheard of occasion for the development of knowledge. Behind every accident, behind every catastrophe, and more to the point, behind the integral accident of knowledge, there is an enormous hope for a new wisdom. A wisdom linked to the grandeur of smallness, linked to the grandeur of humility, to the grandeur of failure. I am not going to go into detail. Against the barbaric, the university was born around the year 1000 in Bologna, Rome, etc. I believe that today, the new university, the University of Disaster, goes up against and looks directly into the eyes of the medusa of progress. Progress is a kind of medusa that one must look at directly with a mirror. So, I agree with you that there is an unheard-of chance. Moreover, I wouldn't have written what I have written if I were without hope. I wouldn't write. I don't know what I would do, but you see what I mean.

Wolfgang Schirmacher: I agree with your last observation. (Progress is a kind of medusa that one must look at directly with a mirror). Because when I speak of wisdom, I am not speaking about a scientific wisdom. I am talking about Socratic wisdom: know thy self. Who am I? Am I my travels? Am I my speculations about other planets? Or am I the being that can spend three hours listening and reflecting? — To have an inner life. Jean Baudrillard, you know in his death notice (which he wrote himself) it reads "existence is not everything; in fact it is the least of things."

Paul Virilio: Well, concerning Baudrillard, I believe that there wasn't much we agreed on. Like the saying goes, we don't have to agree to get along. Jean was a great friend. On many points, we were in complete disagreement. Well, you have understood I am a Christian. That is to say, I don't believe in death. And Baudrillard didn't believe in life, that is the reality of life. This is where one gets the idea of simulations. We were both conscientious objectors. Both atheists, but not the same kind: he didn't believe in reality, in particular in its acceleration, and I don't believe in death, that is to say, in cessation.

In my next book, the integral accident has an "apocalyptic" dimension. I remind you that "apocalypse" means revelation. The integral accident is a revelation: of the finitude of the world and not the end of the world. The end, we don't give a damn about that, it's of no interest. The finitude of the world is a revelation and it will become more revelatory. And this revelation, according to me, goes up against the idea of revolution. When someone tells me, you are a revolutionary; I say no, I am a *revelationary*. And yes, I believe this profoundly. I am not apocalyptic; I repeat, the end of the world is a concept without a future. There is no interest in the end of the world. One "boom" and there is nothing left, that is of no interest to an intellectual or a thinker. The end of the world is lame. Baudrillard was in agreement here, the end of the world is a concept without a future. However, *revelationary*, yes I am a *revelationary*, not only in regards to my faith, but also with regard to my work. It is not exactly the same. In grasping the *revelationary*, you will understand tomorrow if we can't understand grey ecology today. Grey ecology is *revelationary*. The revolution participated in a cosmogony, not only because it refers to the astronomic revolution, but because it trained the ideological revolution. And we know full well, that they failed. Those who are looking, waiting for the revolution, have chosen the wrong planet. Myself, I await the revelation. When I say I am waiting, it's a manner of speaking, because I try to work with this revelation, which is not the revealing of the end but of finitude. That is to say, it opens up to us a new type of thought: the magnitude of the thin (*minceur*). "Of the infra-thin" as Marcel Duchamp would say.

You know there was a man who did extensive work on the problem of poverty: Paul Léautaud. He was a rather interesting fellow. At the moment of his death, someone asked him what he felt and he said, "an enormous curiosity." It's the same with me. I am not speaking about death, or the end, but of finitude, an enormous curiosity in the face of finitude.

Because, it is going to concern philosophy, the economy, the proud science of astrophysics, it will concern the best, Mr. Stephen Hawking, for one. I believe there are also scientific accidents that are preparing themselves. Many scientists are beginning to ask themselves questions about time and space. There is an astrophysicist who studies earthquakes who said modern science was interested in matter and that we have to become interested in the nature of time and space. I completely agree with him. It is here that revelation is possible. An immense curiosity: the University of Disaster is this. That is to say, it goes up against this revelation which is beyond the Copernican revolution, beyond Galileo. What concerns us is the interior and exterior of thought which re-establishes the university not based on barbarism, but on the disaster of knowledge. The idea that finitude gives way to a disaster − the disaster of thought itself gives way to a new thought. This goes way beyond me, and this is what excites me, it exceeds me. In the north of Canada there are Eskimos who are called the Inuit. I say we should all become "inouies" (the unheard-ofs) against this integral accident.

I hope this will get philosophy going again, since I find it quite troubled after the death of Deleuze and all the others. Philosophy has been broken in my opinion. It's for this reason that we return to speaking about Aristotle or Plato. We go back to the Greeks. I knew all of them (the French theorists), and I would say that philosophy at present lacks brilliance. We were phenomenologists, and so we decided to hearken back to Merleau-Ponty and his thought. When I made my first speech at the *Collège International de philosophie* in Barcelona, there was a great debate about Heidegger and the Nazis. I told them, I like Heidegger's work fine, but I warn you I am a Husserlian. I am not Heideggerian. I like Heidegger fine, but I am Husserlian. I am a phenomenologist. A dromologist is obviously a phenomenologist. And I believe that today the return to phenomenology is a bloody sign of how philosophy of the 20th century became broken. Consider the impact of Hannah Arendt, or Edith Stein.

Question: The "critical space" series that you created, I believe Georges Perec was a part of that, and I was thinking about Perec's use of certain rules, like the novel not using the letter E, etc. Is his writing an example in literature or writing of a manner of conceiving what you are speaking about regarding the integral accident?

Paul Virilio: Yes, I think so, but one must not separate literature from the questioning of geometry by Benoît Mandelbrot. I was one of the first to write about Mandelbrot in my critical journal. I remember there was a special edition on mathematics. I was asked if I wanted to write something about math. I said math wasn't my thing, and then, I stumbled across the first edition of Mandelbrot's book on fractal geometry, on fractal objects. I stumbled onto the book and I found it fascinating. Then, Mandelbrot came to one of my lectures. We spoke but we didn't talk about the integral accident. Mandelbrot was not well-received in France at the time, and that was the reason why he had left for the United States, and when he came back to France, he was not happy at all at not being well-received. So, it's true that on one hand, we have the Perecian delirium and I accompanied him; I as well am a man of the city, "a man of the crowd" as Edgar Allen Poe would say: the one who is delirious, who hallucinates. There was in effect a literary dimension that we had in common. The first book by Perec was entitled, *Espèces d'espaces (Species of Spaces),* and from there I discovered Mandelbrot and elsewhere that there were geometries that had the same fractal logic. The entire dimensions were no longer a rock. They were fractioned, accidented, pulverized, and it is this pulverization of geometry that taught me about speed and inspired enormously my research in what was called the "critical space." The word "infra-ordinary" is a word that we forged together and then Perec later adopted and used.

Question: Is there a style or a writing that is proper to the accident?

Paul Virilio: Yes, but the accident is such a big question. How shall I put it, we are obliged to make reference to the title of one of Maurice Blanchot's great works, *The Writing of Disaster*. And of course, the exhibition I did at the Cartier foundation in 2003 to study the accident of disaster, was an attempt to enter into this type of writing. But that is beyond me, outside of my reach. That being said, it is true that there is a language of catastrophe, a writing of disaster. But this writing will reveal itself in the University of Disaster at the criss-crossing of all disciplines. It is not just a literary or poetic phenomenon. It is also a scientific phenomenon. Somewhere along the way it was dealt with in the arsenal. The writing of disaster is the writing of strategy and tactic; it is the writing of total war. It is the writing of the kamikaze which we talked about at the end of the morning session. The writing of disaster is that of war, of military intelligence. I know it well; I am a child of war. It is the writing of disaster that I learned during the bombings of Nantes. For me, the disaster is the invention of modern warfare. Past war, civil war, the tumults of origins, these were merely scuffles. Even if a great many people were killed, they were scuffles. We quickly forget how strategy is not only the mother of Greece, but that which thinks the writing of disaster of the other without thinking that this disaster of the other is also its own. So, there is a military intelligence that we are obliged to steer away from its own extermination by the finitude of the world. And when I see the latest text published in *Le Monde* by Kissinger, that we must (denuclearize) rid ourselves of nuclear bombs. After following the rationale of Kissinger and the United States during the cold war, this statement was quite a revelation. It was a revelation that indicated the correctness of a great logistic specialist, one Dwight Eisenhower. Eisenhower was aware of the finitude of the world, of the provisions of oil, of munitions, and of images via aerial reconnaissance. So, for me, if I have entered knee-deep into the catastrophe, it's because I am a child of this catastrophe. I have often said that war was my mother and my father. The destruction of cities during the Second World War was my university. Yes, there is a writing of disaster and it is written in every arsenal. The arsenals, as I have said, have been the academies of disaster.

What I am saying here is quite harsh. It's difficult to be harsh today. There is a really tragic dimension to the state of the world. Our society is founded on tragedy, on the Greek tragedy; it is the foundation of the west. Somewhere along the way, this tragic thought was still looked down upon. Why is happiness a new idea? It is unjust. Now we are in the middle of a return of the tragic. Like the origin of occidental history, as with Antigone, and Oedipus, etc, somewhere there was a return to the tragic and this return is not only found in literature, but in philosophy, in science, in politics, everywhere. So, throughout modernity, the military intelligence we spoke of earlier: it militarized science. The arsenal completely militarized science, and in particular starting with nuclear power and all that has followed. Now, the intelligence of disaster, the revelation of which I spoke earlier, must civilize, re-civilize science. This is to say, to make it come to terms with its exterminating dimension. It is in this sense that it becomes a grand academic project. At the beginning of the year 1000, and not the year 2000, the academy was about fighting against barbarism. Today, barbarism is the barbarism of our progress. Somewhere along the way, the idea of a universal peace must push back against the possibility of total extermination, of massive destruction, against the question of the political function of war. It is obviously an ecological question. At the least, national suicide which could become international, global is favorable to the accident. We're inspired by the Japan of Hirohito in daring the idea of a global suicide. The question of universal peace does not mean a peace in the sense of "everything's all right." It means the principle itself of an art of war is brought into question as is that of science. Finitude brings into question the art of war as well as the art of politics, and the art of philosophy. Here, there is a revelation that puts an end to the history of the art of war. It is from here that we find a new term that interests me quite a lot, dissuasion. They spoke to us of dissuasion during the Cold War. Today dissuasion comes from this situation. It is no longer weapons that dissuade, it is finiteness that dissuades. It is no longer the red white and blue with its bombs that say you did this or that, now we're going

to fire ballistic missiles on you. It is finiteness itself that
dissuades from warlike thinking, and scientific thinking that
leads to war. This is something that is unheard of, and it is
way beyond me. I don't know what to say about it and I'm
proud of not knowing. If I were told that "I knew" as so many
people like to do, that "we have understood localization," this
would be incorrect, for we have not yet understood finiteness,
ecological finiteness.

Question: Does empathy fit in here somewhere?

Paul Virilio: Yes, certainly. It is a term I like quite a bit, and
it's what we are getting to at a certain level. But how should I
put it? Where one finds phenomenology, one finds deception.
When we enter into the perception of events, the perception of
events is other, it is a setting, and here there is much work to
do because here I would say that in the perception of the event
we are victims of what I call tele-objectivity. Empathy, which
is to say, the perception of the other, the perception of the
world, is linked to subjectivity and objectivity. Now we have
developed technologies, with a couple of exceptions, which
idolize tele-objectivity. Here again, real-time is a determining
factor: Google-Earth, tele-surveillance, etc. Thus, we are up
against a type of pathology of perception. There is an illness
called glaucoma. Without knowing it, there is a restriction of
the visual spectrum, and one loses lateral vision. This is
exactly what happens with the screen. Tele-objectivity is a
glaucoma that can bring empathy into question. Empathy is
the apex of the integral visual field. In the here and now, in the
divine perception, and not by way of a screen, of a
microscope, or the screen of a television, there is a very
important element. I am surprised at the degree to which
people are no longer able to orient themselves in life. They
have lost their perception of their lateral environment. They
are not aware of this glaucoma of the screen, of the ubiquity of
the screen. In the phenomenon of orientation, lateralization is
a determining factor. We know very well that when we aim at
a target, we lose the wider field of vision. Today, the target is
us, and somewhere along the way, we have lost the lateral
field. In interpersonal relations this is a determining factor. In

the relations between the environment and space, it is a determining factor. But when I think of the word "empathy," I think of Klee-- you are right, it will be a word that keeps coming up more and more. There is a rather interesting book, *Abstraktion und Einfühlung* by Wilhelm Worringer, you should read it. It shows the relation between empathy and abstraction. The loss of empathy leads to abstraction. The screen leads to abstraction. The book by Worringer really inspired me. I am an old gestaltist. The psychology of forms fascinates me. Of course I don't believe in forms, but the psychology of forms inspired me, the whole school of Ernst Mach, during the 50s and 60s and Wilhelm Worringer's work is what started it all.

Question: If we lose empathy with abstraction, what do we gain?

Paul Virilio: I think if we look at contemporary art, abstraction has not brought us very much. I knew quite a few painters, Matisse, etc. I can't name them all. I was in that milieu when I was very young. So, the quarrel that raged in the world of painting at that time, in particular around Nicolas de Staël who spoke of "gangs of abstraction" which I liked quite a bit at a time when people were speaking of the "gangs of action" against Citroën car insurance, and he said that there was a kind of "gang of abstraction." It is true that this really interested me. That being said, abstraction posed the question of the visible and the invisible, perhaps the great post-war question. The post-war question in art is that the invisible becomes visible: It's tabula rasa. It's Auschwitz and Hiroshima. I myself was touched by this abstraction which was an event of my childhood. When Nantes was bombed, I give you an example: For a child, a village is like the Alps, indestructible. When we see one afternoon in an instant the house turned to rubble, we can no longer look at it. We become conscientious objectors. We no longer believe. I understood that the eternal can disappear in a blink of the eye. So, abstraction is linked to this destruction and the succession of what took place after. Abstraction is linked to war. We cannot understand abstraction, neo-expressionism, without the first and second world wars. The same can be said for surveillance.

Hubertus von Amelunxen: Having read basically everything you have published, I have never understood Art and Silence, because you turn the fundamental argument of modernism, to render visible, you turn it around saying that abstraction anticipated the becoming-invisible of the world of the visible.

Paul Virilio: Yes, exactly. It truly was a historic moment. That is why even though I am a man of figuration, I liked abstraction.

Hubertus von Amelunxen: I am in more agreement with you here now. We will talk more about it tomorrow.

Paul Virilio: What's more, the first machine of acceleration is not the locomotive of the industrial revolution; it's not the railroad, but the photographic apparatus. The machine of acceleration is the machine of vision. It is instantaneity. You see the hysteria about the invention of instantaneity? It is fabulous. Another way to put it, the world was revolutionized by the camera much more so than by the steam engine or by the TGV, etc. And here, this logic today of photography, creates an incomparable value, like that of art, because it anticipated all the phenomena that we have dealt with since the war of Alsace, up till Lord Snowdon, of whom I speak in my last book, a British photographer for the court and ex-husband of Princess Margaret, who said that "a photo is not art, it is instantaneity." So, somewhere along the way, the photograph has become the most emblematic object of all we have described, more so than the fastest motors, etc.

Hubertus von Amelunxen: We will speak about this tomorrow, but I want to speak about the Swiss Rodolphe Toepffer who said in 1841 that photography is the shrinking of the world, because it will bring that which is far off to us, and in this sense it will destroy all the grandeur of the distant that we need in order to build our creative strength.

Paul Virilio: The original machine of acceleration and speed is the camera. When I did a study on speed at the Cartier Foundation, I put far too many vehicles in the exposition. I wanted with these vehicles, to expose what I just spoke about using Ferraris, jets, etc. I was lucky to be able to blur cinematic time with real-time. There was anti-aircraft radar used by anti-aircraft forces during the occupation. I asked that they put in a real-time feed in order to have a real-time feed of information. We had this feed and a program called "Paul Virilio's Happy Days." And for two hours, during the diffusion of this "Happy Days," in the same room we had the scrolling of information in real-time, there was the coup of Boris Yeltsin and the end of Mikhail Gorbachev, live. I was very happy that we had at least captured this accident. Since then, I received a letter from Gorbachev. I was very proud.

Wolfgang Schirmacher: What exactly is the point? Why always discuss things in terms of placement and distinguishing, enough already! Why not say it's great to have both. Universal media, media artists and what Baudrillard meant. Why do we have to choose between one way of perception or another? Why can't we have as many ways of perceiving as possible? Who says that we aren't able to be mighty, whatever? Who says that when you are born the other dies? It will change. The effort to change the world has enriched the world.

Paul Virilio: It does both at the same time. It is the catastrophe of its success. Success is at the same time, its own catastrophe. You know the phrase by Hannah Arendt, "Progress and catastrophe are two sides of the same coin."

Wolfgang Schirmacher: My friend Lyotard, and your friend too, was smart not to attack progress, he uses the word "development." Development is open. It doesn't have to be progress, but it is acknowledged change, no matter what happens. And I agreed and I accept that in everyday life, media tends to replace things, because people do not have the time and energy we need to grow with media. People have to work. But in our work here, we are the artistic-minded people.

For us, every new perception, every new way of looking at things, discovering, every mode of discovery, is great. We don't have any trouble with having 1000 modes of perception. It doesn't mean perception is lost, it is gained. There is change. With your story, what I have a problem with is "where is the good news?" Where is the constructive news? I agree with all of your criticism, but a crisis is also an opportunity. There is something else going on here. Humans will grow to be able, to become much more than human, super-human if you will: Nietzsche, Übermensch.

Paul Virilio: We always come back to the question of "my negativity." While in reality, I am not at all negative. I simply think that we are in the middle of discovering a new dimension in science and knowledge, and I believe that this is the revelation: that the limit is beyond the limit. It makes us take into account that the environment is much more than a geographical or physical environment, but is a philosophical environment as well. I know, I recognize quite well in this question objections which personally affect me. Virilio is obsessed with catastrophe. Virilio is negative. Whatever, but this is false. What interests me is to go beyond the medusa, to not turn away from its gaze. One must precisely confront the gaze of this catastrophe. All that you said, not only do I admit it: I have nothing to counter it with. I am not crying about progress. I am not crying about the despair of the world. I am profoundly excited by this catastrophe. This is what it means to be a *revelationary*. It's to not turn away from the gaze of negativity. One must look at the negativity with a mirror. I know the reasons you have for saying all that, but, how do I reply? If you allow me, I am a little bit tired of this ping-pong. Which is to say, the return of the ball: "Yes, but if you say that, then that means that..." No! It doesn't mean that! What I say is beyond me. And it excites me to be surpassed by this thought. And in this sense you are completely correct. The catastrophe of photography is a wonder. I don't want to suppress cameras. What I am saying is that limits and finitude are at the heart of our history. Whether you call it development or progress, it doesn't matter. The limit is here, and the manner of saying "maybe it could be this or that" is to not look straight into the eyes of the medusa. If all of you are here, it means that you come from somewhere else. You are not French. If you knew how pissed off I am at the French. And yes, it's for this reason that I am happy you are here and I enjoy all that you are saying. But what I just heard reminds me of what the French say. The reason I agreed to do this lecture is you, the public. You – from elsewhere. You – the antipodes. You – from elsewhere. I am telling you this because, if I live in La Rochelle, it's because somewhere along the way, I deserted Paris and the ways of the Parisian victory that lead nowhere. I wanted to say this because this topic is so important and it is beyond me: the state of philosophical objection has burned out. The debate against victory, the *disputatio* itself, I would say, has burned out by its own finitude. Extermination leads to a reconsideration of the philosophical dialogue in all its old forms. Not in order to go against the objection and to ask for a perfect approval, that would be boring. I am half-Italian, I enjoy a dialogue. I enjoy the pleasure of intellectual sport, but I feel that the state of objection is in need of a total reconstruction. How does one pose the objection when confronted with this situation? How does one shift the position of the *disputatio*? In France, I can tell you, it is paralyzed. Since the 1960s, when we had the great liberty of the 60s and Deleuze, Guattari, and Lyotard, we left the Cartesian objection. And all that has burned out. Today it is finished. We have gone in a circle; we have arrived at the old *disputatio*. It is for this reason that I no longer keep up much of a relationship with certain philosophers today. We are not facing the catastrophe; we are faced with finitude. We have not found a way to exchange the contradiction. We have to invent a new relationship between contradiction and objection. This is, in my opinion, the major philosophical question in particular in France. In France, it's terrible. You know as well as I do another expression "one must laugh," because, as Lacan said, "If it doesn't make someone laugh, it doesn't communicate." That's why I said about Baudrillard that we didn't have to agree in order to get along. In France, one has to be in agreement in order to get along. Yesterday, understanding was the art of arts; today, one must guess. This changes quite honestly the status of the dialogue. This is very important in my opinion.

Question: Can you give us a case of how we could respond to this situation?

Paul Virilio: Like I said earlier, I am not correct. I can't be correct; today the question is open. The arrival at the limit, at finitude is a situation of openness that surpasses philosophical and political thought today, including my own. That is why the debate in France about Cartesian reason is completely old-fashioned. It is completely outdated. The phrase of our generation, how does one adhere to this? For example, "One must give the finitude of the world." We don't understand it. We will understand in "X" number of generations when we will have addressed the question of finitude. It is the revelation of the end of the world, of the finite world. Yes, there is an overcoming of the traditional concept of reason which will throw us into a delirium of who knows what. But from the work of the philosophers of the 60s who appeared to me delirious, I think of Guattari for one. Did they know an answer to the situation of the overcoming of reason and the traditional statute of the dialogue and objection, etc.? The situation is open. At this moment we are launching "open sky" accords for transatlantic transport. But what is open is precisely the question of finitude. The question of finitude surpasses our comprehension, our art of understanding with which we constructed the last 2000 years. This is, as well, the crisis of the university. The university is the inheritor, since the year 1000 of this construction of the dialogue of contradiction and objection throughout different thought. We are on the verge of a considerable event. The accident of knowledge, the accident of traditional comprehension, I would say, is an event that exceeds us. If you are ready to enter with me into this excess here, we can continue our dialogue. If for traditional reasons, you turn your back on the question of contradiction and of traditional debates, we cannot advance into this open world of the end. The world of the end, of finitude, is an open world for science and for thought. This is the accident of science.

The accident of knowledge is an unparalleled event. It is an element without a reference. The accident of substance, etc. we can find in Aristotle. But here, I am speaking to you about the accident of knowledge. And the paltry words I use in trying to explain this accident to you aren't up to the task. They talk me up. If I told you I was right that would be absurd. Everything I said would be absurd. This is the magnitude of poverty. There is such a power, such a revelation, that one cannot be up for the task.

Session III
Art as far as the eye can see

We can understand the statement by Karlheinz Stockhausen who said that the greatest work of art in history was ground zero. Three thousand bodies…it's logical. And then, it was shown around the world on television. It was shown everywhere and forever. It is the chef-d'oeuvre of death: the falling of the bodies. I want to begin with a small introduction in relation to the dialogue that we had yesterday with Wolfgang (Schirmacher) because it opened my mind up to something I will develop elsewhere: Why the dialogue and the *disputatio* are important. Today the status of objection, of critique, of the *disputatio*, changes. We do not engage in dialogue. We do not debate in the same manner if we are in a lifeboat, an amphitheatre, or a classroom. You see already the modification of the debate for television, with the swiftness of the exchanges. This disrupts the content between the presenter and his aptly named "guest collaborator." [sic] I call this type of debate "ping-pong." "You have five seconds to respond." "Ping-pong." The limited character in time of the present situation, the present situation of the host, conditions the content of the dialogue. When I go on television, I hate it. I have Italian roots and I want time to speak. I do not want to play "ping-pong."

Regarding this situation of the dialogue, what we call empathic phenomenology opened dialogue, but dramaturgy imposes its anti-empathic constraint. We are going to speak about two aspects of art: war, and obviously, instantaneity: two aspects that condition the blind spot of art. The First World War was mundane. The Second World War was total. They were not at all the same. This war (the second) was to integrally condition art and western culture. Art, in western culture, is a victim of war. The question then becomes, is art an invalid or invalid? I think this is very important because art has a dimension which triumphs over criticism. Each time I discuss with an art critic, they tell me, you're an art critic, but you don't like art. The problem is not to like it, but to observe what it is, what happens to it. And here I will give you a very simple example. The first phase of relativist impressionism, more than cubism, introduced Einsteinian relativity to expressionism, Otto Dix, and all the expressionists. What happened between the two wars? Following the commune of Paris, the war of 1870, Expressionism arrived after the First World War. Expressionism was the first wound, the first handicap of art. Then, we had surrealism. We can't understand surrealism, "the magnetic fields" of André Breton, and Louis Aragon without the wonder of the fireworks of war: The explosives and the gas. And after the Second World War, we had Actionism which we don't speak often enough about. We can't understand art today without Viennese Actionism. And in doing this of course, in passing by abstraction, we have lost sight of the figure. The non-figuration of the stand-in is the deportation of art. I repeat that the Second World War was marked by the deportation of populations, but also the deportation of art from Europe to America. It was an event of war. We cannot understand the transference of influence of European art, which was the avant-garde, towards American art which we'll call contemporary art, without the deportation of war. We deported the Jews, we deported art. Another aspect that conditions the blind spot of art is speed and instantaneity. I said yesterday that the instantaneity of photography, then cinematography, and finally becoming real through television, with the imperialism of immediatized real-time is something that injures contemporary art. Contemporary art has become less temporary and more fatally intemporary. This is a very important word. Contrary to contemporary art, there is intemporary art. Namely, art has broken with its historical filiations. Which is to say, contemporary art is in accidental rupture with the origins of art. I am going to read a small excerpt from a text I wrote, because it summarizes this very well. At the beginning of 2007, the director of the Contemporary Museum of Modern Art of Vienna asked me to write a small text about the art programmed for the year. I will give you a brief excerpt.

"In the 19th century with impressionism and its pheno-menology, it was the freedom of impressions that was released from academism. In the 20th century with expressionism and its dramaturgy, it was the freedom of expression which liberated itself from conformism. In the 21st century, today, these two freedoms of mind threaten to disappear when confronted with the acceleration of a digital reality which erases everything, including all representational memories. Against this, the Museum of Contemporary Art of Vienna could become the improbable conservatory, at least, of the unexpected: the museum of the accident of "real-time"."

In order to better confirm what I am saying here, the word transfer is very important. The "transfer" from analogy to numerology; I prefer the word numerology to digital. I remind you that numerology was a religion. This is very important. The transfer from analogy to numerology, what we call digital and its photographic software, etc. passes from representation, a distance, a memory, to pure representation. It is real-time. Realism, the hyperrealism of real-time, the hyperrealism of America, moreover, anticipates pictorially the situation I call tele-objectivity. The American hyperrealism that Baudrillard loved so much was introductive of the hyperreality of acceleration. Photographic instantaneity was the first machine of vision and the first machine of acceleration of instantaneity, much more so than the gun. The photograph is the initial case in the acceleration of reality. It will lead to the birth of cinematography, which is to say, to the cinematic parade of images. It will render visible cinematic effects. We have forgotten that the cinematic was the energy of the visible. There is kinetic energy with accidents, movements of the body and impacts, but there is also cinematic energy. In this way, the recording chamber of a camera is much more important than the machine of acceleration which is the locomotive that revolutionizes transportation. With cinema, photography will revolutionize transmission with the television and tele-surveillance in real-time. Thus, starting from the crisis of instantaneity to live telecommunications, we will witness not only the acceleration of history, but the acceleration of reality itself. Presentation in real-time of things, of objects, of events, will supplant the old representations of real space.

Presentation in real-time is going to supplant the representation in real space of pictorial, sculptural, or architectural works, to the point of putting contemporary art under wraps which, beginning with abstraction, spreads the blind spot of art in mixing all the aesthetic disciplines of history. Thus, next to the object and the subject, objectivity and subjectivity, there is the technological phase which will bring forth what we can name without a doubt: tele-objectivity and its emotional tele-subjectivities. The entirety of this situation comes from the energy of the visible. This is a phrase I like a lot: the energy of the visible. From the filmic sequence and the photogram, all the way to the tele-visual videogram, all in addition to the kinetic energy of modern modes of transport, there is the cinematic energy of the means of transmission. So, kinetic energy is found in all modes of transport, the TGV, airplanes, etc. But with cinematic energy, no one recognizes cinematic energy as energy: namely, the cinematic energy of transmission. Transportation is linked to a kinetic energy. Transmission is a cinematic energy that is both audio and visual.

In fact, like the political economy, the economy of culture suffered two lashings: not only the acceleration of art history as we mentioned, in the 19th century, but also starting not very long ago, the acceleration of reality, thanks to the progress of the information and communications revolution in real-time which definitively disrupts the real space of forms, of sculpture for the benefit of real-time and the rhythmology of image and sound. (Rhythmology here replaces morphology.) It is for this reason that I say contemporary art, or rather intemporary art and its morphology, suffers from the assault of quasi-musical rhythmology. I repeat that music is the origin of speed. Contemporary art and its morphology suffers a quasi-musical rythmological assault from diverse performances and installations mixed together more and more in what we call "the living spectacle."

We find ourselves in the struggled mourning of an art of light, of the speed of light, of illumination, en route toward the becoming-music of the televised image. One must choose between the dynamic and its emotional panic, and the trance state of the subjugated crowds. This is music, including military music. It is here and nowhere else that the political economy plays itself out.

Wolfgang Schirmacher: I need to understand you better. Why do we have to choose? Because the point is, I could make a great case for not choosing. Why can't we allow both to exist? Why can't I say, "Today is Tuesday, it will be my body day, tomorrow is Wednesday, it will be my mind day?"

Paul Virilio: That's freedom. When there is no choice, there is no freedom. Myself, I am an architect. Never forget that I am an architect and urbanist and not at all a philosopher. I hold onto forms. I will end in saying that the fate of the democratic political economy, I remind you, and I continue to remind distinguished economists, that the fate of the world depends not only on the political economy of wealth, but also on the military political economy with the music of the march. It is here that we find how the political economy of democracy is linked with the political economy of speed. Today we cannot speak about all this without a grey ecology, that is to say, an ecology of the acceleration of reality. The futurists understood, and the futurists were what? Fascists. I am Italian. I admire Marinetti, but in my opinion, the futurists introduced fascism. I am a victim of the blitzkrieg.

Question: Is it not correct to see light and matter together? Being an architect, do we not put the dynamic with the static?

Paul Virilio: Architecture furnishes the matter to an instantaneous and simultaneous collective reception of materiality.

Question: I am thinking about the relation between emotion and abstraction. On the one hand, there is the transcendent side of a divine transcendent light of power, and on the other hand there is the immanence that resists this transcendence which opposes power. Can we put all of that together?

Paul Virilio: I cannot answer this question. I can't answer this question, because as I said yesterday, the situation is open. It is open. I have not figured out what I am telling you. I don't say this out of modesty, but out of realism. We have spoken about this since the beginning: The work that I do is an approximation. Here we are in the middle of the essential question. There needs to be a considerable amount of work done in order to have an answer to this question. This being said, I can even speak of the community of interests of the traditional political economy and in democracy and the community of emotions. We have here two worlds which are radically different. The community of interests is linked to the political economy of wealth, to the social state, to socialism, to communism. While the other side, the world of democracy, of the democracy of emotions, is linked to the speed of emotions. That is to say, to something innate: emotion, and the first emotion: fear. Fear is the pure power of emotions. It is an innate emotion and, thus we come face to face with a politics, a community of emotions that cannot be democratic.

Tomorrow we will begin to standardize not only opinions, as has been the case for products, but we will also begin to standardize behavior. We cannot standardize emotions without synchronizing them. That is to say, without occasioning that everyone thinks the same and feels the same emotion at the same moment: real-time. Here we are outside of democracy. We are in an ideality. We are up against a phenomenon that puts an end to democracy. The democracy of reflex is not the democracy of reflection. The conditioned reflex has nothing to do with reflection with others. It is an enormous task that will be done in the University of Disaster. Another way to put it is to call it the "globalization of affects in real-time."

Question: Being against fascism and in favor of democracy, I want to ask you, as a human, a man, which makes me a subject, and as subject under democracy, I have rights: Is art a right? (Virilio nods yes.) That being the case, I want to talk about the tele-visual problem of which you spoke. Since the beginning of photography, the materiality of photography has left a residue behind and this is called an archive, for

*example, of paintings like the large archive here in France.
There are hundreds of thousands of paintings, images,
drawings, and sculptures that have never been seen by the
public in a democratic society. What would you say if we used
this technology that you seem to be against to allow people to
see them and to disseminate them around the world?*

Paul Virilio: I have absolutely nothing against new
technologies. To put it another way, some people say "Virilio
is a technophobe." No, I am not a technophobe. I am even a
user of new technologies. I have tried to explain to you that
what is essential is the path to finitude, finitude and not the
end. We see the archives. What is the finitude of the archive?
If we don't speak of the finitude of the archive in the period of
globalization, we shouldn't speak of the archive. What is the
finitude of the archive? It is the "Library of Babel" – the short-
story by Jorge Luis Borges. So, the question that poses itself
today with the library of Babel is that in the possibility of
achieving its success, it ultimately fails. We always return to
the idea of finitude, that its success is perhaps its failure: that
plenitude can become finitude. So, it's not about denying the
importance of the library of Babel. It's about studying today,
due to real-time, globalization in its finitude. The moment that
we have studied this accident of finitude, and return to the
tower of Babel, and then to the library of Babel, we can then
begin to speak of the archive. Today, we can no longer start at
the beginning and go toward the end. We must start at the end
and head toward the beginning, because the end is here. The
finitude of all art, and the world, is here. Finitude is in front of
us, and we must start from the end, not in order to cry, "Oh,
it's horrible." No, we must do this in order to confront the end
and be able to go beyond it. I don't know where this will lead,
by the way.

*Question: Are you saying that the global dissemination of art
digitally would continue the process of blinding the vision of
the viewers due to the acceleration and overabundance that
can lead to finitude?*

Paul Virilio: I cannot answer this question, because it is beyond me. The moment we reach the finitude of globalism, we enter into megalomania or megalopsychia. This is why I say I do not have the answer. It is out of modesty, out of realism. No one, not even Einstein, Hawking, or Plato can master globalization. Those who say, "Hey guys, I've found the answer!" are a joke. I do not master globalization, and it's an honor to not master it. It's my strength. That is to say, to be merely a man. Contrary to this idea, I read a book by a scientist named Joel de Rosnay who directs La Cité du Science in Paris and who is fascinated by what? The global brain. He speaks of a global brain which will be the continuity of all brains. I think this is a horror. It is the communist name for the collective intellectual. I will give you an example. During the Vietnam War, I had a Vietnamese student who became a professor, and who lived through the Vietnam War against the Americans. He told me that it's extraordinary, the collective intellectual worked so well against the imperialists. Every time we had any type of problem, we sent a messenger by bike who explained what the problem was. It could be a problem of water reduction or repairs, etc., and the communists, in eight to ten days, would send us an answer. The Vietnamese collective intellectual found an answer, hooray!

Question: When you speak of a pitiless art, I have the feeling that you are speaking about this in a negative form. That you call for an art that has pity. It reminds me of Nietzsche's critique of pity as a way in which the object of pity becomes frozen into that form. Do you mean pity, or would you equally use the word empathy or sympathy in allowing for a becoming of pity?

Paul Virilio: That's a big question which has a small answer. We keep coming back to the same thing: the two orders of magnitude of Bossuet. The magnitude of power can be pitiless and unforgiving. The magnitude of poverty is full of pity, pitiful. The two orders are linked. Good and evil no longer exist. So what! Here we begin to touch upon the question, and I do touch upon this question via space-time. I am not saying this is bad; it's good. But here we find the increase in the order of magnitude of power and the order of magnitude of poverty, of weakness. A world which denies, as was the case during World War II, the order of magnitude of poverty, of weakness, is a world that is finished, that has exhausted itself and leads to what? – global suicide. It leads not only to a national suicide, which was almost the case in Japan which I spoke about earlier, but a global suicide. The kamikaze is in a certain way the hero of this world without pity. He is even without pity *vis-a-vis* himself. It is not just a passive suicide, where he says, I am suffering, I can't do it any longer, but an active suicide: I want my death to make the whole world die. We can no longer function with this order of the magnitude of power. That is what we call finitude. This is the current situation in the world of ecology.

In starting from the position of the end, of finitude, we can re-pose the question of art, the question of empathy, of morals. Here there is a situation that is beyond us, which is beyond me, because I am of the order of the magnitude of pity. That is to say, of the *misericordia*. The *misericordia,* compassion, is often considered a weakness. It is a power, that of weakness, and we cannot get rid of it at the risk of nourishing a collective suicide like that of the Japanese, or America regarding Hiroshima. I will give you an example of the magnitude of poverty and the magnitude of power. This glass is at its absolute magnitude of power. It is as big as it can be. If the glass were three meters tall, it would no longer be a glass; it would be a water tower. Weakness, pity is a power. I will give you one more example. I took part in a conference, and there was a young medieval historian who spoke of the pitiless and the pitiful. He compared women to the knights in the Middle Ages. The women called their knights, "gentle knight." Another way to put it: He was pitied. Why? In the sexual rapport he was not without pity. I remind you that the knight of the Middle Ages was a real butcher. For the woman, it was not her knight that she bestowed pity upon but her "gentle" lover. There is something very profound here. The word pitiful is not used in the proper manner. You see? The word pitiful means, without pity – ah! But here, it's the other way around.

Question: Who is going to finance the University of Disaster?

Paul Virilio: I am not militant enough to inaugurate the University of Disaster, nor the Museum of Disaster. The University of Disaster is a book. It's what I call a message in a bottle tossed out to sea. My books are messages in bottles sent out to sea. I have no pretensions of inaugurating this university. But I know that today, the individual intellectual, not the collective intellectual, is what? He/she is something that moves between the role of spin-doctor, director of communications, or in the area of the secret services, an agent of influence. I am nothing more than an agent of influence. I am not paid by the KGB or the Palestinians or the like, but I consider the political intellectuals, as once existed in the world of Sartre, gone. The time of an intellectual having an influence is over. Who has an influence? It is the climate.

Question: Can the accident be literature? I am thinking about the fugue and music. Can the accident also be art as well?

Paul Virilio: The integral accident concerns all the forms of civilization. The accident is the succession of poetry, the continuation of the novel, the continuation of history, of biology, of astronomy. Ok, if it takes us 50,000 years to go to other planets, this is the accident of astrophysics. This is the integral accident. The integral accident is integral. It covers the accident in all disciplines. This is why there is the university. The accident is universal and involves and implicates the university in its finitude. It is an event that is beyond us, that is beyond me, but which together, we can confront. Together means each person in their own time. Of course, of course, this is an event. Accidents have replaced events. The speed of real-time, the acceleration of reality is such that accidents have become events by virtue of their position, by their acceleration alone. Events are the unexpected. In a certain sense, past authorities waited for the event. We are going to have a war, ah, here it is. You wait for it, or you don't. Now, you don't even have time to wait. Things arrive without waiting for them. It is this that is the accident, it is that which happens. The acceleration of time is also the acceleration of the event. The event comes from the accident. The attempts on 9/11 were attacks in images of an accidental event. It is an extraordinary event, because it replaces war. There is an element that one shouldn't forget. There were close to 3,300 deaths. There were two planes that were taken over, etc. and there were, I don't know, eighteen men in the plane, I don't know the exact number. I remind you that in order to achieve the same destruction – 3,000 deaths and an impact as big as that – it took the entire force of the Japanese navy: aircraft carriers, battleships, fighter planes, to cause the death of 2,000 people. Their death unleashed the war in the Pacific. On one hand, we have an event which took time. There were many things that happened between Hirohito, the American president, etc. And in the other case, bam! There were eighteen young men with two commercial airplanes, and this is nothing next to the nuclear possibilities of an accident involving the whole world. So, the acceleration of reality in accelerating all events becomes the question of history. There was an anthropologist who said, "We are nothing more than anthropologists of the present." We are no longer the anthropologists of history, of Charlemagne, etc. We are merely anthropologists of the present.

Question: Adding on to what you are saying: Art is no longer the accident. We are moving toward a new generation of artists where they are trying to prevent the accident and using art as a preventative art. When I talk about this, I am specifically referring to gaming. In producing art in order to see what's going to happen, you are anticipating the event in order to prevent the event. So, I think we are suspended. I think if art moves toward the accident while producing art and making the accident happen, we will find solutions for many of the questions we are asking.

Paul Virilio: Guessing. This is getting at what I said before. Yesterday, understanding was the art of arts. Now, one must guess happiness, guess sadness. Guessing. It's not the avant-garde of art; it's waiting for the unexpected.

Wolfgang Schirmacher: The point is, in gaming, just by pretending that they embrace the accident, they are preventing it from happening. So it is already a control of the accident.

Paul Virilio: Most machines of simulation, I'm thinking of military simulators, flight simulators – it's a simulation of a bizarre conduct. The simulation is not a normal operating procedure. One learns the standard operating procedure in the plane. In the simulators, one simulates catastrophes very well, and the time of normal flight and the time of the simulator are identical.

Wolfgang Schirmacher: But the word is out. The artist today knows that what is good for the marketplace is good for the accident. But they are not really exposing themselves to any accidents. They are already simulating this control.

Question: Could there be a re-grasping of finitude or a certain logistics of perception through a mise-en-scene? Looking to Baudrillard in relation to thinking, Baudrillard said that it might be virtual reality that saves reality. Could we construct a representation of a more humanized technology and possibly de-militarize the tools of the military?

Paul Virilio: The big difference between Jean and me is that he worked on simulation and I worked on substitution. I chose substitution in saying that there were periods of the real as there were periods of history, and that simulation, via a proverb or literature, whether it is literal or not - take the advent of perspective in Renaissance painting - simulation leaves the place for a new real. For example, the Homeric simulation of oral literature passed into reality. The great artists of literature simulated magical, mythical situations which became completely real and banal. It is the same with the car. It passed into reality in our time. Today, it's the same. The informatics simulation is no lesser or greater than the Homeric oration or the grand fantasies of Leonardo Da Vinci.

So, for me, what interests me is the phase of substitution, it's the moment in which reality changes. It's not the moment it is simulated by one art or another, but the moment reality installs itself in the place of art. In my work, we are in the middle of simulation, but for me, the question becomes what simulation will reality pass into? In what order of reality will we find ourselves? Only for me the substitution is an instantaneous phase. The important thing is, when does this substitution become real? I will give you an example of this perspective. For me, the intention of perspective, the *camera obscura*, is an element created by political history. Perspective is inherently a political and urban phenomenon, and it modifies everything. Machiavelli and the cities of the Renaissance did not come about by chance. The political economy of this period didn't come about by chance. Thus, the perspective of real space was an extraordinary moment. I am talking about the perspective of perception and not simply that of the canvas. No, I see in relief before I see in relief, or rather, I didn't know that I was seeing in relief. I see in relief without knowing it. To see is not to know. Today, if I make a substitution of what you just spoke of, then I think we are going toward a visual perspective of real-time. How? We are moving from a real space perspective one moment toward a real-time perspective. We are not yet there today. We have not yet reached the phase of substitution. What is the real-time perspective? It is what I call a stereoreality. What is stereoreality? It is the sharps and the flats, and it gives off a "ping," a sound relief. Stereo-real, stereoreality: I have at my disposal the vision of the moment, in action. I see you. I am with you in real space, the object is in front of me, and on the other hand, I have the actual-virtual vision which replaces the sharps and the flats. I have a field of vision that gives me a relief of perspective other than that of the relief of the Italian Renaissance: The stereo-temporal and stereo-spatial relief. This I believe in very much, and this is why I am not against screens and I am not a technophobe. It's a new relief.

I would like to relate a small anecdote about Baudrillard and simulation and substitution. When we found ourselves at the

Revue Travers, I had just finished my photographic campaign, which took ten years, on the wall of the Atlantic. Baudrillard hated photography at the time. I went to the *Revue Travers* because before, in the *Revue de L'esprit*, they didn't have photos or images. At the *Revue Travers*, I could publish my photos and I told the revue, "I am coming." When I saw Baudrillard, he said, "Tisk, tisk, tisk." And now, he is dead and I am still alive…It's been quite a long time now since I have stopped taking photos, but he, he began taking photos. He even finally became a photographer. This is typical in our movement.

Wolfgang Schirmacher: A young artist asks you today, what should he or she glean from your philosophy? What is your advice? You don't have advice, but if you had advice, what would it be? My understanding is that we are in a world of globalization and the acceleration of speed. This is our situation, but it is a situation similar to fate in which the artist cannot help but join. As an artist you can resist and find other possibilities, different material ways of doing it. And that is actually being aware of what is going on, not denying that this is happening, but also not saying that this is a fact, I have to join.

Paul Virilio: Ok, I am going to make a reference to a great philosopher who was also a doctor of the church: Augustine, St. Augustine, who along with Heidegger spoke best about time. He had a phrase which goes something like this: Do whatever you want, but do it with love. Piety, pity – having pity, not necessarily a religious pity, but a pity. If you do it with love, with pity, then you can do it. If you do it without love, without pity, you become pitiless, and then don't do it. This is the magnitude of poverty. This is philosophical love, philosophical pity. It is not necessarily religious. If you do it with love, then you can do it; if you don't do it with love, then let it go, because in that case, it's already ruined. Earlier, we spoke about the knight, the knight who has pity. We spoke of San Francisco, but I forgot another one, Don Quixote, one of the greatest knights of pity in the history of literature.

Question: I wonder what you think about the enormous number of students who imagine they can go to art school and become artists, and end up just producing bad art. I wonder if this has something to do with your ideas of acceleration and proportion. It makes us more finite as teachers and lovers of art.

Paul Virilio: This is a problem of violence. Speed is absolute violence. Speed is the violence of all violence. So, in a sense the problem is not to slow down, it's about taking a step back, in order to better jump. Step back, in order to go farther, that is to say, to create some distance. In any art, one must find the focal point. You shouldn't accept the event head-on; one must always take a step back. Take a step back, like in boxing, in order to spread out the impact. Recoil in order to spread out. This is not against violence or speed. Speed is the hypertrophy of violence. I give an example. If your cheek is against mine, with the same hand I can caress it or I can slap it. What is it that makes it a slap? It's the development in space of the focal point; otherwise, it's a caress. So, make caresses. Take a step back; one shouldn't be violent, it doesn't serve anything. It is the kamikaze. What is at stake today is the K – not that of Kafka, but of the Kamikaze. I spoke yesterday of the pollution of distance. Do you remember, the pollution of substance is green ecology? The pollution of distance is grey ecology. One must keep one's distance. It is from here that we get the idea of keeping what is called the extension. Never allow yourself to be cornered like a boxer on the ropes. When we are cornered, we are screwed. One must always turn, as when dancing in order to maintain the distance. It's this that doesn't pollute distance.

Question: What is your idea of transience? Don't you think that dromology belongs to the transient? What is the place in dromology for the fugitive?

Paul Virilio: It's the contrary of Heidegger: "All grandeur is in the leap." The fugitive is taking a step back. I think what we need today is to take a step back, a step back for victory and not for the end. "All grandeur is in the leap." This is

Stalingrad, Verdun. The magnitude of poverty is to take a step back in order to confront, to cope with the problem. As I said earlier, a boxer takes a step back in order to gain distance, in order to maintain a distance. With the kamikaze, all grandeur is in the leap. He arrives with his explosives, and you are all dead. This is Heidegger. All grandeur is in the leap. For the *puce*, for the pious and those with pity, it is not like this. It is the step back, in intelligence, in distance. There is no intelligence without a step back, without re-presentation. That is to say, without giving oneself to the focal point of reason. In the leap, the individual is without reason, is unreasonable. It is the end of the hero in the traditional sense of the word. Today, in the contemporary world, the last hero is not Don Quixote, but rather the kamikaze. And I say it is Don Quixote. And you as well....if you are artists, you can't be kamikazes. It's for this reason that I can't tolerate actionism. It prefigures the kamikaze, the one who puts an end to his life and the world. This could be a general who pushes a button, or the pilot who drops the bombs on Hiroshima.

Question: I think there is a relationship here with precariousness.

Paul Virilio: Yes, precisely. The magnitude of poverty is the magnitude of precariousness. "If I am nothing, then I am everything." It's the opposite of Marcus Aurelius. "I was everything, the emperor of the Romans, it is nothing." Today it's: I am nothing, and this nothing is everything. This is the step back, from the pride of the leap of the knight. Siegfried or Don Quixote. That reminds me of a really good book by Milan Kundera called *Le Rideau (The Curtain)*.

This manner of speaking is what we call the *contre-coup*, the recoil. It's very interesting. When we devour an end, a finitude, the history of the world devours the finitude of geophysics. When we go up against an end, a wall, we recoil. This is called a kick-back, a recoil. One doesn't need to recoil in order to take a step back. For example, when one shoots a gun (I was a soldier in Germany), it hurts, above all when one is using a 50-30. Ecology is this recoil. It is the magnitude of poverty, which is itself a recoil in relationship to the end. Everything, I would say, is sketched out in the notion of finitude. We have reached the finitude, and thus, it's in relation to this that one can think, complain, etc. It's not sad.

Wolfgang Schirmacher: That's exactly what Heidegger said.

Hubertus von Amelunxen: The poverty of thought is the effectuation of death.

Paul Virilio: That's not Heidegger. This being said, I have a great respect for Heidegger. Listen, the history of Heidegger and Nazism, I have a desire to say to the world: A great philosopher, a great painter, can also be a monster. Caravaggio, for example, was a great painter and an assassin. One can be a great philosopher, and politically, a monster. I am not saying that Heidegger was a monster. Just because he was at Freiburg when the Nazis came to power, does not mean that he wasn't a great philosopher. And when I speak of Caravaggio, people say, "How horrible, he was an assassin, and thus, his paintings must be monstrous."

Question: I had a question about this transference from representation to presentation. To me, this seems like Aristotle's differentiation between variation in drawing, between mimesis and diegesis. My question is, can dromology function as a type of theatre?

Paul Virilio: Of course, dromology already participates in the *mise-en-scene* of the world. It replaces the transparency of the space of things, the transparency of water, air, glass, by the trans-appearance of time. Tele-perception is a trans-appearance of real-time, while the glass is a trans-appearance of the glass. And there is something quite precise here: the notion that transparence evolved with the acceleration of real-time. In reality, when real space dominated instantaneous time, transparency was of a material form: water, air, glass, fog. With the arrival of real-time, we entered into trans-appearance. It is an appearance that is instantaneously transmitted from a distance by virtue of real-time. One is an appearance by virtue of the real space of the atmosphere; the other is the trans-appearance of a transmission. Speed participates in this *mise-en-forme* of trans-appearance. This is why I speak at the political level of the trans-political. We are at the level of the tyranny of real-time. That is to say, in the acceleration of reality, we are in the trans-political. Trans-appearance is the speed of light.

Question: With the acceleration of transmission, can you speak about the replication of images?

Paul Virilio: The introductory text by Walter Benjamin, *Art in the Age of its Mechanical Reproduction*, has taken on considerable proportions with cloning. The great danger of the uniformation of the world is cloning; not only of images, but of being, through genetics. It's an integral conformism. Which is to say, we enter into a logic of velocity where everything is re-doubled to infinity as in a mirror that re-doubles images. So, the conformism of modernity is much worse than academism with its standards and looks, styles, genres, fads which for a certain time, reign. Here, there is a possibility of a unique model – not only what we call politically correct, but optically correct. There is nothing worse to imagine than the optically correct. It is this that haunts me with the possibilities of reproduction of not only images, but of situations, of standardizing situations with synchronization. This is where I would say we get the failure of success. For me today, celebrity is really dead. I am not saying this out of modesty because I am a phenomenon. No, I say this because someone who is famous in his system of conformism is of no interest.

Zidane is a great soccer player, I don't give a shit. Shakespeare was a great philosopher and writer. Why is Shakespeare famous? He participates in the trans-historical celebration. I have nothing against Zidane, I could speak of Madonna, whomever, it doesn't matter. In a certain way, celebrity is dead in the name of celebration. Before, celebrity was an individual, a clever one, who all of a sudden made a difference in whatever domain. Today, it's the celebration of a standard, be it a media star like Zidane or a big philosopher like Bernard Henri-Levy. For me, it's finished, done. I will give you an example: Henri Michaux (I could cite others, but it doesn't matter). Michaux: no interviews, no photos, never, he was silent. He existed by the silence and withdrawal in relationship to the trans-apparent illumination. We see the same thing with Thomas Pynchon, a great contemporary writer.

I am going to tell you a story about a great French cartoonist, Jean –Louis Forain. Forain was a comic cartoonist and he was invited to a great exhibit of the painters and cartoonists of the 19th century. He arrives, looks at the cartoons, he contemplates and then he splits. An artist sees Forain and says, "Monsieur Forain, Monsieur Forain," and he sees the face of Forain (which is not very excited by what he sees) and the artist says, "You have to earn a living." And at that moment Forain says, "To do what you do, I don't see any interest in it." This is very interesting. He didn't criticize him. He didn't appreciate it, and he had nothing to say, and he said nothing. The artist who comes and says, "You have to earn a living." It's not a question of having a means to live, but a means to survive. The question isn't whether he liked the drawings or not, it was that the painter justified his drawings by the fact, "I need to earn a living, so I do this."

I will give you another example. When I was really young, practically none of my friends lived off of their art or creative work. None. They had a second job. For example, I won't cite anyone, but I know pretty much all the great architects in the world. I am very worried right now by some of them who have great talent because they have developed their magnitude of power. They have developed their own firms with 150 designers. It's colossal. The result is that they cannot do what they want to do. In order to keep their agency, they are obliged to do a little of everything. And little by little, they lose their terrain, and they have never been as famous as they are right now.

Question: Can you speak to the question of separation and projection of identity online?

Paul Virilio: In my opinion, it's an illusion of freedom. Man and woman are unique, like fingerprints. We know this from DNA and fingerprinting. Technologies are not only going to permit cloning of the identical, but also the technification of difference. That is to say, I come from a family, a tribe where I am an individual. In my opinion, it's the diaspora of freedom, the dispersion of freedom. In the realm of the theatre, this is completely recognized. It's part of the theatre: the actor and his double. At the level of the social theatre, in my opinion, we enter into a dramaturgy which is the loss of identity. There is a loss. There is an acquired skill, but with the risk of losing oneself. There is a phrase by Christ in the gospel, "For what will it profit a man if he gains the world but loses his soul?"

In hearing what I say here, it doesn't mean that you shouldn't play, that you shouldn't have your avatars, etc. It's not forbidden. It means that you should pose the question all the way to its limit. It's always the same question: Up until what? What is the limit of role playing? If we don't pose the question of the limit, in my opinion, we can't play. If we don't pose the question of the limit, I think that we become depersonalized.

Question: Can you speak a little more about your link to Max Stirner?

Paul Virilio: I was a part of the people who were interested in anarchy, above all when I was young. When we have a little bit of freedom, we are interested in anarchy, above all when we are young. And thus, the question of the uniqueness of being is such an obvious question that the fact we are obliged to justify it today, shows to what point we are already disorganized, in decomposition. In May of '68, I was part of a group of people who tried to shake things up at the Odeon theatre. The first sentence I put forth from the stage of the Odeon was, "We don't compose with a society that is in decomposition." Another way to put it, I was already sensitive to the fact that anarchy is about decomposition.

In May of '68, there were two places: the Sorbonne for the communists, and the Odeon theatre for the anarchists and the situationists. For example, I remember being in one of the great lecture halls at that moment in '68, and someone with a glove of a very precise color got up on the stage saying, "I just read on the walls that imagination has seized power." And I screamed, "That being so, you are denying imagination to the people." It was a gesture of youth.

Question: I am trying to tie together a few things that you said this morning and this afternoon about art and politics. You described a situation where we are moving from the regime of representation and something else is taking its place. I don't think it's necessarily just presentation, because that is just a falling back somehow, but perhaps it's the rhythm of the process of the presentation in real-time, the synchronization and globalization of real-time. And I see this as kind of a resonance. So maybe we leave a regime of representation for one of resonance.

Paul Virilio: Of course, we are obliged to make the oppositions of presentation/representation, the real space of time on one hand, and the space of real-time on the other. Obviously, it's not about intervening with the presentation, the accidental effect that changes everything, the key word, etc., it's not about evacuating. The distinguishing element of real-time is its position to dominate. It is not real-time that is dangerous, but it's at the moment that it becomes the most important time of presentation, where all the rest is discriminated against. The danger is not speed and absolute violence. The problem is not speed, it is that it becomes more and more supported and that "live" representation, instantaneity, dominates definitively the time of representation.

We know quite well that there is substitution. We can see it happening right now. I will give you an example. When we create a technical object, we eliminate another. For example, there are no longer any typewriters. I type; well, it's my wife who types for me. I am not so talented when it comes to that. There are no longer any typewriters, there are only computers. I am sorry, but horses still exist. The big issue today is, tomorrow there will no longer be any horses, only cars. Tomorrow there will no longer be the handling of texts, and no longer any pens. The problem is dominance. It's the same problem I spoke of yesterday regarding science. I said that science is economizing. It discovers in the same way we discover a continent. Then it exploits the continent, and then it leaves. This exploitative dimension of science also exists in technology. What I fear is not presentation and its resonance of representation. That is part of musicality. My fear is that the power of conditioning of the absolute speed of light will be eliminatory.

I will give another example. In the transmission of transportation, when we get out of our cars, we're not forced to get out on one side or the other. We don't have to drive a car. Do you agree? We can walk. But if we continue like this, we will no longer be able to walk. This is true with regard to the order of technology. The means of transportation which are my legs is taken into account by the car that transports me, but I can put it in the garage and go for a walk. In the same way, riding a horse is really nice. The danger is that one day we will no longer be able to walk because there will only be escalators, moving walkways, and such. Because there will be a special engine that realigns my mobility. One must not forget the possibility of elimination through progress: Progress can be eliminating. If progress doesn't eliminate something, there is no problem; it's a plus. People ask me, "How can you write on a typewriter, that's ridiculous." What right do you have to say that? That pisses me off! I like my typewriter. I say, who has made the typewriter forbidden? Who has banned the pen? I send letters and manuscripts written in pen, and I remind you that there are autograph sellers, that Victor Hugo wrote letters which were sold for hundreds of dollars, but when I write a letter in longhand, people tell me, "Really, you don't have much respect for me." Ok, you want me to type you a letter with a machine. Do you see the discredit taking place here? This is, according to me, elimination by progress.

At the school where I taught, I started an informatics laboratory. It worked so well that even the Metro-Parisians sent their workers to it. As for cars, I have a magnificent Jaguar. It is fast and I like it that way. Yes...yes...the dynamism of the technical...who survives this?

Question: I wonder if I understand the difference between intemporary art and contemporary art.

Paul Virilio: There is a very good quote in my book on art: The dialogue between Auguste Rodin and Paul Roussel, when Rodin calls out to a man who is walking. Rodin was interested in the mobility of the body. He was interested like Giacometti, at an important moment when a man walks. And Paul Roussel defended the instantaneity of the photo in saying, "No, your guy there; this is ridiculous, do you see how he walks?" And Rodin says, "No, because in reality, time doesn't stop. And in my sculptures, I have taken into account the duration of time. That is why I modified the position."

In looking at this figure (sculpture) we see time pass, the time of walking. It's not simply the instantaneous time of the photo. It is the same in the paintings of Edgar Degas when he makes his race horses. The hooves of horses don't exactly correspond with reality. It's very difficult to see the hooves of horses. We had to wait for Eadweard Muybridge in order to see how to position the hooves of the horse. There is a great debate between the time that passes and the time that stops. The real-time of instantaneity is a time that is arrested. It is not arrested in a fixed sense, but arrested in the sense of the flowing of time. It's complex and at the same time, it is very obvious. For someone who has done sculptures and painting like Degas, it is understood.

I would like to distinguish between the intemporal and the intemporary. The intemporal is what arrests time, with its instantaneity. And I say that intemporary art is that which breaks its filiations with the past arts, from the Renaissance to classicism, etc. The whole history of art is nothing but a long tracking shot where the different phases of art are linked together. Starting with the 19th century, with the industrial revolution, art cut itself away from its filiations. Intemporary art is the art of cutting the ties with its filiations. It is a disaffiliated art. This neologism, intemporary, shows that we cannot be contemporary because we inscribe ourselves in modern history.

Question: Has the photo become the original sin?

Paul Virilio: The first vision machine that started it all is the camera. One can't understand generalized tele-surveillance without the camera. For example, at this moment in London there are 3 million surveillance cameras, and each person is videotaped three hundred times a day. All of this came from "klick, klack, Kodak." The progress of speed is also the progress of elimination. Speed is linked to racing. Racing is the progress of elimination. The concourse is a competition and elimination. It is the magnitude of poverty.

Question: We know that history is written for the winners and you speak of the magnitude of poverty which is so essential. What means do we have in front of us to make this position valuable?

Paul Virilio: We have the means in front us, that is to say, for the latest elimination, the biosphere, we have grey ecology. What is eliminated by speed is the earth. The environment is eliminated at the expense of searching for an exotic planet elsewhere. When we say externalization, to eliminate, it is not only the elimination of horses in relation to cars, or the typewriter in relation to the computer; it's that the earth is too small for the provocation of speed. The earth is reduced to nothing. Another way to put it is that it is reduced to the magnitude of poverty by the acceleration of the provocation. It is from this that we hear already the provocation by great scientists that "we must go elsewhere." If we want to survive, it's Stephen Hawking. We must find another planet. That is philosophical madness! We are in a world of madness. Science has become an operative science and no longer a science of knowledge or wisdom. What we call techno-science is a farce, due to its success in eliminating the earth. Not only by pollution in ecology, but by the pollution of distances and time. The scale of the world has become the miniaturization of the world, and that's unthinkable. Someone who says that is a madman. Not a madman in the sense of Michel Foucault and others who spoke of the alienated, but in the philosophical sense. These latest Darwinians who say, "Eliminate the weak. It's the earth that has become too weak for progress. Too small, too ridiculous, too lost. We have to find another earth." This is pure madness. It is megalopsychia and no longer megalomania.

I am thinking about the comments in the French newspapers by Nicholas Hulot's that the French presidential candidates should absolutely have a meeting on global warming and the problem of pollution, and, at the same time, the scientists and astrophysicists are speaking about the necessity to find another inhabitable planet, it doesn't work. It is either one or the other. There is an absolute contradiction there. Science cannot search for an inhabitable planet to colonize and at the same time tells us to save the planet. There is an absolute contradiction in this. The grand science of astronomy which was interested in the earth, suddenly tells us, careful, the earth is polluted, we should preserve it, and then in the same instant tell us that well maybe we could find an inhabitable planet 50,000 light years away. Here, there is madness. You cannot speak of ecology at the same time as exo-planets. It's about the here and now!

Question: I am interested in what you said earlier about love, regarding how the artist should position his/herself. And I am thinking about Jean-Luc Nancy's idea of the gift – of giving a gift without expecting something in return. So I guess my question is, is love an accident?

Paul Virilio: Certainly not.

Question: Of course, love is not an accident, but can we not also look at art as we do love? Is there a movement of art that is an "in-accidental art?"

Paul Virilio: Yes, there is no substance without an accident. Accident and substance are two sides of the same coin. Hannah Arendt tells us that the miracle and the catastrophe are two sides of the same coin. I will give you an example: Airbus: 800 seats, 800 deaths. So, there is no substance, no distance without accident.

Question: I would like for you to speak to the question of absence, which is present with the accident. It's like non-being.

Paul Virilio: No, it's like a sleeping conscience. We are awake to the extent that we are asleep. We are alive to the extent that we are mortal. Those who say, "I don't want to die," cannot be alive. If you can't be absent, then you can't be present. The two are linked. The waking state, one must speak of the gash of sleep, and I am not capable of that here. You have to talk about Freud and the paradox of sleep. Sleep is a world apart. Night and day, we have before us a logic of being that is visual and obscure. The waking state is presence and absence. My only professor of morality was my cat. I was nine or ten years old. I was at Nantes during the bombings. We were in the streets and there was a cat that belonged to a merchant. I loved this cat and this cat loved me. I told him, if it gives you pleasure, I will pet you. He always got in a position to be cuddled. I loved this cat so much, that I started to caress it all the time and then it scratched me. He was right. He was fed up. That is morality. This poor cat, it's not privation. It's too much is too much. One must make a break. One must caress it, and then leave it. There must be a break.

PART II: Critical Response

The Aesthetics of Resistance

Jason Adams

While much of the attention directed towards Virilio's *ouevre* derives from his confrontation with the "properly" political, perhaps the most important source of resistance to which he returns throughout his work is that of the aesthetic. Like Heidegger, he argues that that the ancient ecology of *techne* was concealed by the instrumentality of technique and that this will be revealed in the long-term unfolding of the arts. But unlike Heidegger, Virilio is alive in a time in which this legacy has been forgotten, over the course of the past century of the development of contemporary art, which leads him to be very critical of the broad swath of it. In this period in which the empire of speed was set into motion, he argues that there has emerged an "aesthetics of disappearance," one that has uncritically converged with technique and supplanted the aesthetics of appearance that Heidegger had seen as a possible source of divergence from it. As Virilio explains, with the latter, "There was an enduring material support to the image: wood or canvas in the case of paintings; marble in the case of sculptures...but with the invention of photography, of the photogramme, that is of instant photography, and of cinematography, from that moment onwards one enters into an aesthetic of disappearance...things owe their existence to the fact that they disappear." This is an important point because to a great extent this history of the convergence of art and technique mirrors that of the atrocities of the twentieth century, in which the most powerful states owed their existence to the fact that millions of "bodies-without-souls" were forced to disappear; "I would even say that Nazi nihilism introduces this question. The death camps were an attempt to bring on this disappearance. I think this feeling of perfecting disappearance is there among the dangers of the virtual. We would be confronted with a kind of negationism, a virtual one denying the reality of bodies, of the earth, of the mind." While this may sound extreme, Virilio points out the

importance of peering into the abyss even if one does not
choose to believe what one sees there; what he has seen, he
tells us, is that contemporary art has lost its emancipatory
potential and has become complicit instead with the destruction of the body. "These days when people get down to
debate the relevance or awfulness of contemporary art, they
generally forget to ask one vital question; contemporary art,
sure, but contemporary with what?" The weight of this
question is confirmed for him in the reflections of the aesthetic
theorist Jacqueline Lichtenstein, who upon visiting the
museum at Auschwitz had the terrifying feeling of being in the
presence of images from contemporary art, leading her to
lament that "they had won, since they'd produced forms of
perception that are all of a piece with the mode of destruction
they made their own." However, while much contemporary art
conforms to this aesthetic, Virilio affirms that as with
technology more broadly, there have also been exceptions to
it, as seen in the divergence between what he calls "pitiful"
art, which embraces the aesthetics of appearance, the
conviviality of bodies and "popular defense," and what he
calls "pitiless" art, which embraces the aesthetics of
disappearance, the de-struction of the body and the terrorist
assault; "Terrorism isn't just a political phenomenon, it's also
an artistic phenomenon. It exists in advertising, in the media,
in the reality show, the pornographic media...after the end of
abstract art, after all those people who were still people of
culture; we have stuttered the horror revealed by Auschwitz
and Hiroshima." Virilio takes this critique so far that he even
dismisses radical artists such as the Dadaists, Futurists,
Surrealists and Situationists with whom he has often been
associated, as being complicit due to their collective embrace
of an aesthetic of pitilessness. For example, he points out that
this can be seen in the frank statements in support of total war
and "revolutionary" dictatorship made by Hulsenbeck,
Marinetti and Breton, just as it can in the defense of sadism
and random killing in Debord. A similar pitilessness is seen in
such recent examples as what he describes as "the truly
decisive step" when Gunther von Hagens opened his *World of
Bodies* in Mannheim, Germany with the intention of "breaking

the last remaining taboos;" the display featured 200 plastinated corpses, "standing tall like statues of antiquity, the flayed cadavers either brandished their skins like trophies of some kind or showed off their innards in imitation of Salvador Dali's *Venus de Milo With Drawers*." Virilio saw this as akin to the pitiless aesthetic of Ilse Koch of Buchenwald, who turned the skins of extermination camp victims into lampshades and other "taboo-challenging" pieces of the early twentieth century; indeed, as he quotes of an anxious art dealer of that time, "The new German painting, naturally, represents current sensibility in Germany...furious, murderous demoniacal heads – not in the style of the old masters but in completely modern manner: scientific, choking with poison gas."

Clearly then, the Nazis were not alone in their pitiless aesthetic, for just as they embraced photography and film in the battle for hearts and minds, so too did the Soviets with their penchant for "Socialist Realism" and the documentary film; although it is generally overlooked, Virilio points out that this is also reflected in the West by the British Documentary Movement and "Mass Observation" which he says emerged largely as "a reaction against the art world." Thus for Virilio, the reason photography and film were so revered by these regimes was that they contributed to the pitiless de-struction of the lived experience of the body, rather than forming a balance between them. Since the speed of the shutter was far quicker than that of the human eye, it was supposed that this allowed it to escape the "mere subjectivity" of human perception and to replace it with an objective, scientific account of the world; as Virilio elaborates, "considered irrefutable proof of the existence of an objective world, the snapshot was in fact, the bearer of its own future ruin...the more instrumental photography became (in medicine, in astronomy, in military strategy) the more it penetrated beyond immediate vision, the less the problem of how to interpret its products managed to emerge beyond the déjà vu of objective evidence." Thus for him, interpretation is always at issue, since not only is there always some body

behind the camera imposing their view upon the world, but the
very form of the camera itself is imbued with the values of the
culture that produced it; therefore in the midst of a pitiless age,
"it is art that tells the truth and photography that lies. For in
reality time does not stand still...duration is automatically
defeated by the innovation of photographic instantaneity, for if
the instantaneous image pretends to scientific accuracy in its
details, the snapshot's image-freeze or rather image-time-
freeze invariably distorts the witness's felt temporality."
Although he maintains that it is the hierarchy of speed that
mobilizes photography, Virilio does concede that none of this
would have come to pass had it not been for the tendency of
the visual arts – including aesthetics of appearance such as
painting – to become transformed into *logos* (as occurred with
the *Mona Lisa*), whereas with other art forms this was not
necessarily the case. "While theater and dance – those arts
involving immediate presence – still demand prolonged
attention, we sum up the visual arts immediately, or as good
as. The very recent development of real-time computer
imagery only ever accentuates this effect of iconic
stupefaction." Many of these same feature are found in film
medium, which not only "puts a uniform on the eyes" such
that the entire audience views the work from the same
perspective (as opposed to the multiperspectival quality of
theater), but eventually even destroys the early features of
analogue, silent, monochromatic film, replacing these with a
perceptual regime whereby the digital, the sonorous and the
multichromatic prevail. The tragedy of this "progression" is
the de-struction of the imagination and interpretation that had
originally given art its phenomenological character, thus
allowing prosthetic perception to take over from bodily
perception, rather than being in league with it. As Virilio
observes, "nowadays everything that remains silent is deemed
to consent, to accept without a word of protest the background
noise of audiovisual immoderation...no silence can express
disapproval or resistance but only consent. The silence of the
image is not only animated by the motorization of film
segments; it is also enlisted in the general acquiescence of a

total art – the seventh art which, they would claim, contained all the rest."

Yet it would not be long before this assumption would be proven presumptuous with the appearance of such phenomena as "transgenic art" such as that produced by pitiless artists like Eduardo Kac, who create a totally artificial universe, splicing the genes of dogs, rabbits, fish, plants and amoebas with Green Fluorescent Protein simply for the amusement of watching them glow green. Virilio's reply is that this is not, as some have argued, a new category of art like any other but is instead the destruction of art in its entirety, achieved by attacking the very root of its appearance; as he explains, "Transgenic art is renewing the other arts from the inside. Because its focus is the map of the human genome. And we can't treat genetic science as just another science in parallel with the others. It is inside all of the other sciences. It is a way to focus science on its source – the living organism and the knowledge of it...[thus] it exterminates the source of the other arts. The living organism is irreplaceable. The living organism is not of the same nature as what produces it." As Virilio sees it, transgenic art is nothing less than the example *par excellence* of the late modern complicity between art and technoscience, a convergence that has been organized in such a way that the former has already lost its specificity so as to be redeployed as one more element of the digitalization of everything that exists: as he puts it, "The instrument of number is preparing to dominate the *analogon* once and for all – in other words to dominate anything which presents a resemblance, or relations of similitude, between beings and things. This leads, self-evidently, to the denial of any phenomenology. Far from wishing to 'save phenomena' as philosophy demanded, we shall henceforth have to mislay them, to lose them beneath calculations, beneath the speed of a calculation which outstrips any time of thought, any intelligent reflection." Thus the unmeasured aesthetics of appearance becomes subject not only to the calculations of the scientific expert whose accumulation of information sets things into motion, but also those of the corporate sponsor whose accumulation of capital opens the door to its realization. One example of the latter that he gives is that of "a power powerful cosmetics multinational [that] recently formed partnerships with the Palazzo Pitti and the Barberini to co-produce art shows and participate in the 'restoration' of old works of art which will, we are told, be readapted to current tastes." Such instrumentalizations of the "old masters," while clearly reflecting the nihilism of transgenic art, are also he claims, not so distant from the assertions of artists such as Stockhausen, who has forthrightly proclaimed that the WTC bombings were "the greatest work of art ever." For Virilio, statements of this order are not so much evidence of the transgression of the confines of the old order as they are evidence of its deepening through the insemination of contemporary art with the totalitarian version of the dictum "beyond good and evil": not only beyond morality, but beyond ethics as such. Thus in light of the emergence of transgenic, digital, corporate and terrorist art, he argues that the outcome has been the destruction of the body that is its basis (or at the very least its partner): "The art of the motor – cinematographic, video-computer graphic – has finally torpedoed the lack of motorization of the 'primary arts.' And I don't just mean the oceanographic arts or those that have come to light at Thule in Greenland but also, equally the gesture of the artist who, first and foremost, brought his body with him: *habeus corpus*; all those corporal arts whose vestiges remain the actor and the dancer. Such motorization thus prefigures the disastrous virtualization of choreography, the grotesque dance of clones and avatars."

While photographic, filmic and "biological" art all conformed to the pitiless aesthetic of the de-struction of the body so too do the so-called countercultures that express their divergence largely through the mediums of clothing and music. In fact, as Virilio sees it, the primary elements of such milieu, including baggy clothing, piercing, body modification, scarification, tattoos and heroin in punk, hip-hop and rave, all revolve around the de-struction of animal, social and territorial bodies, which is why he refers to them as "counternature" rather than "counterculture." The popularity amongst all of these crowds

of combat boots, army pants and coats begs for him the
critique of the soldier's costume, which emerged in an attempt
to camouflage himself from the perceptual prostheses of the
enemy. "During the war of 1914 the authorities agree on the
evident advantage in renouncing bright colors in the
manufacture of uniforms and in adopting a habit of neutral
shade to diminish the visibility of troops in the field...they
picked sky-blue, field gray, gray-green, and finally English
army khaki." By the time of the first Gulf War at the other end
of the century, the camouflage suit has been largely replaced
by the antichemical suit, a costume which he sees as having
features in common with the bodybag, appearing everywhere
from Mardi Gras festivals to the runways of Paris. Thus over
the course of the century, "Not only have the beautiful
sparkling uniforms of wars past disappeared forever, to be
replaced by the khaki work clothes of the soldiers; but now the
dappled combat uniform has also disappeared into a wrapping
not so different from a garbage bag." Despite the distance
between these sartorial transformations, the underlying theme
that has remained for both is the importance of hiding the
contours of the body behind the veil of sameness; this is
because, as Virilio has it, "the disappearance of the body's
characteristics in the uniformity of the civil or military dress
goes along with the disappearance of the body in the
unidirectionality of speed." In fact it is for this reason that for
contemporary countercultures, "Music is the art of reference,
that is, an art of time and acceleration. It's an art of time and
speed. It is even the first to have given form to speed. It's not
by chance that young people only have one art, and that's
music." Yet while music is based on the aesthetics of
disappearance, in his characteristic, ultimately affirmative
fashion, Virilio points out that it is in fact a holdover from a
time when the aesthetics of appearance were still dominant,
meaning that not all forms of music are equally pitiless;
indeed, he points out that he has been a jazz enthusiast since
the Second World War, when it was the music of the
Resistance. In addition to this, Virilio argues that jazz
possesses more of an aura of proximity to it than
contemporary popular music; as he elaborates, "The

destruction of jazz by rock was a very significant moment of deconstruction. The process of subjectivization in jazz is based on alterity. And to have alterity, you need two bodies. Hence the jam session. In rock though, the link with alterity is broken. People have ended up dancing on their own."

From the basis of these critiques then, it can be inferred that a "pitiful" aesthetics of resistance would be one that would mount a popular defense of the body, of alterity and of the aura of the original piece, since "what, at first glance, distinguishes the true work of art, as Rainer Maria Rilke wrote, is its 'infinite solitude,' the enigmatic attraction of a uniqueness which, paradoxically, offers the multitude of its sensory adequations to those who, in looking at them, produce half the picture." Which is why he sees Impressionism as having been such an important form of divergence when photography was first being introduced; as he explains, "for one brief moment Impressionism – in painting and music – was able to retrieve the flavor of the ephemeral before the nihilism of contemporary technology wiped it out." So, instead of the valueless embrace of acceleration, individuation and violence, Virilio argues that it is time to reclaim the legacy of artistic resistance as seen in pitiful artists such as Debussy, Coltrane, Monet, Bonnard, Chaplin, Dylan and others of this ilk, "It is once again necessary to diverge. It is necessary to become a critic. Impressionism was a critique of photography and documentary filmmaking a critique of propaganda. So today we have to institute an art criticism of the technosciences." Just as "Joyce, Beckett and Kafka were writers who diverged writing" even amongst what he would call the typically pitiless artists of cinema and television, there have been those who have subverted the primary function of the medium, including Wiseman, Rosellini, Godard, and Loach. Thus while he may be largely negative about the emancipatory potential of technique in the production of art he clearly does not write it off altogether and it would be absurd to assert that Virilio is simply reductionist. However, although he has conceded the possibility of divergent music and film, it is no secret that the primarily interest is in art forms which he sees as reinscribing the animal, social and territorial bodies within the *hic et nunc* of being, since as he puts it, "To think about the here and now, the temporality and presence of art, is to oppose its disappearance, to refuse being a collaborator." Therefore what is closest to an aesthetic of resistance is that which emphasizes the importance of corporeality even in the midst of its disappearance, "Since art has already left its spaces and begun floating through the worlds of advertising and the media, the last that resists is the body…that's why I'm in love with bodies. I think that alongside 'SOS save our souls' we should invent 'SOS save our bodies from electromagnetic electrocution.' Art forms that he emphasizes in this regard include dance, theater, painting, sculpture, land art and architecture, those forms that have always been the bases of the aesthetics of appearance. One playwright who he has influenced in this sense is Heiner Muller, who both diverges film and reinscribes theater at once; "Here is a theater that really plays with the deferred time of video: you have a video receiver that functions as a rear-view mirror, letting the spectator see something other than what's to be seen on the stage." As for dance, Virilio points to Sergei Diaghilev, emphasizing that he had told his dancers to 'astonish' him by rejecting the banality of the machine and embracing the fluidity and spontaneity of organic life instead; this is important because "the work of art is not academic; it conforms to no preconceived plan and expresses only the extreme veneration of receptiveness or, more trivially, of the extreme vigilance of the living body that sees, hears, intuits, moves, breathes and changes." Thus he argues in favor of bringing back an aesthetic that could intersect meaningfully with a politic of real space over (or at least on a level with) real-time, one that would privilege proximity and communication rather than alienation and mutual silence while also drawing attention to the biggest question of our time, that of the body and its de-struction by the empire of speed.

One particularly outstanding example of this is seen in Virilio's longstanding project to curate a "museum of accidents," which would embrace the aesthetics of appearance since it would expose the hidden nature of technological substance. But as he sees it, up until the museum is actually built, television will remain the closest thing to a museum of the accident since it really is the only "place" where we come into contact with its effects on a regular basis. In other words, since television exists in real-time rather than real space it is therefore based upon an aesthetic of disappearance, which means that the accident is still largely hidden to us. For instance if one goes to any of the hundreds of "museums of science and industry" that dot the American landscape in real space, one finds that while the technology is everywhere apparent the accident appropriate to it has been censored. It was toward this eventual goal that Virilio put together an exhibition at the Fondation Cartier in Paris, accompanied by the book *Unknown Quantity*, which consists of large-format photographs taken from the mainstream press, of the major accidents of the 20th century. In doing so, he effectively re-inscribed these fleeting images into real space so that they could be comprehended and contemplated in a way that would otherwise be unlikely. The exhibition and book can thus be seen as equivalent for the general public to what the simulation industry is for government and business; a medium with which to "expose the accident in order not to be exposed to it." "This is the very point, the avowed aim of the Fondation Cartier exhibition. A pilot project for, or exactly a prefiguration of, the future Museum of the Accident...[which is important because] as one witness to the rise of nihilism in Europe put it, 'the most atrocious act becomes easy when the path leading to it has been duly cleared." In this sense, then, the exhibition *Unknown Quantity* can be understood as a direct challenge to those art forms that have become little more than propaganda for the empire of speed such as "transgenic art" or "implantation art," in which the artist advertises the "liberation" of the body by torturing and altering not only her own body, but often those of others as well, with or without their consent. Thus, just as astronomers have recently begun to plan ahead for the next collision with "near earth asteroids" such as that which impacted Tunguska, Siberia in 1908 or Flagstaff, Arizona several millennia ago, Virilio argues that his project is no less serious, since "accidents always reveal something that is indispensable to knowledge. You can't create the positive without creating the negative...that there are negative monuments for me is an extraordinary advance [because] negative means that we remember in order not to do it again."

Works Cited

J. Armitage, ed. *Virilio Live Selected Interviews* (London: Sage, 2001)

M. Heidegger, *The Question Concerning Technology* (New York: Harper Collins, 1982)

P. Virilio, *Art and Fear* trans. Julie Rose (London: Continuum, 2003)

P. Virilio, *The Vision Machine* (Bloomington: Indiana University Press, 1994)

P. Virilio, *Crepuscular Dawn* trans. Sylvere Lotringer (New York: Semiotext(e), 2002)

P. Virilio, *The Information Bomb* trans. Chris Turner (London: Verso, 2000)

P. Virilio, *Ground Zero* (London: Verso, 2002)

P. Virilio, *Aesthetics of Disappearance* (New York: Semiotext(e), 1991)

P. Virilio, *Desert Screen: War at the Speed of Light* (London: Continuum, 2002)

P. Virilio, S. Lotringer, *Pure War* trans. Mark Polizotti (New York: Semiotext(e), 1997)

P. Virilio, *Politics of the Very Worst* (New York: Semiotext(e), 1999)

P. Virilio, *Unknown Quantity* (New York: Thames and Hudson, 2003)

La Bombe Philosophique: An Archaeology of the Stereoscopic Present (or, Sporting Through the Shrapnel)

Sean Smith

Albert Einstein's hypothesis of three imminent bombs—nuclear, information, population—is a motif that has woven its way insistently into Paul Virilio's analysis of contemporary society and his war model of urban change. It is an astute conceptual choice for Virilio since it was in the twentieth century that the implications of light speed and the theory of relativity continually unfolded to reshape social relations from the local community level to that of global geopolitics, punctuated most resoundingly by the twin detonations of Little Boy and Fat Man in 1945, and those of the Twin Towers in 2001.

That said, the seductiveness of the bomb as motif proves problematic at times since Virilio himself weaves between the traditional understanding of a weapon and his true interest, which is the idea of bomb as metaphor for the accident that is located within the substance of any technology. Semantically fusing the weapon with the accident obscures those aspects of intent and agency required to instrumentalize properties of the latter for creating and detonating a bomb of the former type.

The relationship between war machines and accidents is complicated as the question of property enters the discussion, for in the post-Fordist regime we find that *all* types of information have been rendered to the property form. Here is the point at which Virilio's genetic bomb emerges from Einstein's population bomb—not because of the expressly militaristic imperative as before with the Manhattan Project and ARPAnet, but because of the profit potential that exists in owning the language of living things and creating flesh products based on that knowledge. This should not be understood as a recourse to dialectical materialism but rather an exploration of how the trialectic relationship between weapon, accident and property form may suggest new lines of inquiry for the questions that Virilio poses.

Little Boy to Fat Man might also be understood as the consumption trajectory of Western sport masculinity, from the promising young athlete to the just past prime spectator of television. In this trajectory the dynamics of the libidinal yield to the stasis of the lipidinal as the nervous system accelerates faster than what is capable by mere flesh and bone. Dromology, of course, has its root in the Greek word *dromos*, for race or running, that most fundamental of sporting cultures. And whether we are discussing the Olympian sort with its *citius, altius, fortius (...copiosus)* or the commodified professional sort of capitalist accumulation, sporting cultures are at their core grounded in moving bodies which have been subject throughout their history to forces of acceleration. They might thus play a role in helping us understand a logic and politics of speed, how speed is created, how it is administered, and the accident that lies within.

Perhaps none of Virilio's many contributions to critical thought are so visceral as the detonation of this philosophical bomb of bombs. As such, they beg a visceral response. With that in mind, consider the following an attempt to catalogue an archaeology of the stereoscopic present—a present in which we simultaneously exist in the corporeality of the everyday with its sensuality, affect and duration, as well as the global real-time of the network in which light speed has telescoped all past and future into a persistent now. And if the notion of a catalogue seems far too linear for the age of networked optoelectronics, then instead consider the following a form of speed writing to match that accelerating shockwave which Virilio has exploded all around us.

.011 Stereoscopic Illumination

Virilio once said in interview that he always has an image in mind when beginning to write. From surface to line, the image acts as a primer for the words that eventually flow across the page. In our case it is two images that illuminate and inspire this frantic attempt at speed writing, each positioned side by side. The first is of a fireball blooming out of a skyscraper on September 11, 2001, a dark and brilliant flower of flame and smoke and ash that resonates in a very corporeal fashion with the televiewer even today. The second image, only slightly less familiar than the first, was taken five years earlier. It features the American boxer Muhammad Ali, his tremblings from Parkinson's disease frozen in time as he lights the flame at the opening ceremonies of the centenary Olympic Games in Atlanta. Two images, two flames. As the mind's eye relaxes the two images begin to merge, almost stereoscopically, to suggest the outlines of a third image, which…

.021 Symbolic Architecture

…though Virilio boasts the architectural pedigree, it is Baudrillard who frames the devastation of 9/11 primarily as an inquest into the form and function of the World Trade Center buildings. While this symbol of American economic power is indeed paramount, we cannot forget that the Pentagon and White House, symbols of military and political power, were hit as well. (Though the latter was not actually hit by an airplane, most media reports in the immediate aftermath indicated that is where the terrorists were headed. Zacarias Moussaoui's testimony years later only confirmed this belief after the fact.) Perhaps in some way blinded by the light of the burning towers, both Baudrillard and Virilio give short shrift to the other two targets on that day, but this is a mistake. It is the three targets taken together that constitute the message: an engagement of the American hegemonic forces blazing the trail of globalization by striking at the trio of architectural forms that symbolically defined the nation *in extensio*.

.022 The Overcompressed City

Hollywood was the first great project of the industrialization of information compression, a folding of entire buildings and cities into a few square miles of gated Los Angeles suburb. Notably, its nine massive hillside letters were cleverly positioned just out of reach of the other three great American landmarks destroyed on September 11. While economic, military and political symbols were each struck that day, it was the entertainment symbol and all that it had represented at the frontier of westward expansion that gave the semiotic *raison d'etre* for their destruction in the first place. From expansion to compression, for if there is an information bomb of the nuclear sort it is not only because the vectors of transmission have enveloped the earth in near-total fashion, but also because the compressed density of information in contemporary exchanges is such that *explosiveness-in-potential* trembles deep within...

.031 The Nuclear Information Bomb

...the detonation of a nuclear fission weapon is a two-stage process. The first involves a conventional chemical explosive blasting outwards in a relatively controlled fashion. This sets off the second stage, a series of exponentially growing chain reactions in fissile material that ultimately reaches a supercritical mass and becomes the nuclear detonation, what Virilio described as destruction at the speed of a camera flash. Two speeds, two blasts, one devastating outcome. The planes hitting the World Trade Center during the 9/11 attack would be considered relatively conventional weapons in the historical lineage of projectiles launched at architectural forms. But if thought of in analogy to the nuclear bomb they become the chemical primer of an assembly that only thereafter reaches the supercritical second stage...

.032 Medium + Message

...of the 1993 bombing of the World Trade Center Virilio discusses a mutation in warfare, driven in part by the combination of truck bomb and news report, which he suggests vectors us towards the solo agent as a new form of political economy. But the 1993 attack was a failure. It wasn't until the 2001 attack on the World Trade Center that Terror showed evidence of lessons learned, ironically, from the Americans during the First Gulf War: the use of camera-equipped smart bombs, which transmitted images to CNN of approaching targets before vanishing to static in a unique merging of medium and message. A more poignant example of Virilio's new political economy was achieved by the terrorists on 9/11: camera and airplane, though spatially separated, were part-objects in the same assemblage of destruction.

.033 Instant Replay

Baudrillard reads the World Trade Center bombings under the sign of closure: two majestic towers standing higher than the rest, facing inward to each other and closing off the potential of the semiotic. But this reading is possible only so long as we can consider them in an isolated vacuum of signification. Once the camera is introduced to the architectural form—and most in the 9/11 audience had never seen the World Trade Center in person—any such semiotic closure must be opened anew. The dromological understanding of this re-opening may be located in the mediated consumption of athletic bodies in motion, that of the *instant replay*. The caveat here is that the visual dynamics were reversed: instead of a mediated replay serving to illustrate the preceding live event, we had an anterior replay of a plane hitting a building better preparing us to witness the live event of the second plane making explosive contact...

.034 Absolute and Relative Speed

...Virilio's dromology concerns speed as both an absolute quantity and as relative qualities of intensity. It was the *slowness* of the planes that made them a particularly useful weapon that day. As opposed to the truck bombs used at the World Trade Center in 1993, which exploded so fast that television *was only able to capture the damage done*, the slowness of the airliners on 9/11 allowed one to position a personal video camera in time to view the plane striking the tower—in other words, *to witness the actual event taking place*. It was only at this point of supercritical mass that speed accelerated to the absolute real-time of the kinematic image, the nuclear-information detonation delivering an experience far more tactile and visceral than seeing the rubble after the fact...

.035 Interactive Decay

...many of those caught in the blast wave of the 9/11 information bomb had never actually seen the World Trade Center in person nor contoured its architecture as a sensing subject. Instead, their understanding of the buildings was that of doubled signifier: first, as the symbol of American economic might and the attendant conquest of neoliberalism on a worldwide scale; and second, as the sign of *authentication*, in which stock scenes of the two towers were routinely spliced in with footage shot on Hollywood soundstage or on location elsewhere to establish the principle of New York-ness. As a salve for the trauma inflicted by the terrorist salvo these stock shots were removed from many information archives following 9/11. Only a few years thereafter they were restored to their original frame sequences, though, perhaps offering us a source of empirical data to determine a half-life of interactive decay.

.041 The Acceleration of Duration

...the destruction wrought on 9/11 Baudrillard wonders: What
architectural form is worthy of being annihilated today? In
considering the question we must first acknowledge that any
potentially targeted architectural object must carve out a
unique figure in both space *and* time. That a building should
be distinctive enough in its spatial form and purpose is
obvious, but an element of duration is also required for that
object to have accumulated the requisite symbolic capital
necessary to achieve a critical semiotic yield. This is what
makes the case of the World Trade Center particularly
interesting: in only three decades, the Twin Towers were able
to absorb all the symbolism of an American capitalism that
had ambitions of radiating globally. Put differently, the light
speed of Hollywood and the spectacle-making industry *had
accelerated the process of forging duration.*

.042 Olympics as Duration

...the quadrennial period of the Olympiad provides a cadence
that complements the everyday rhythms of dwelling and
commerce. While the Olympics are a periodic and spatially
nomadic athletic carnival, they temporally persist even after
any particular event has ended. Speed (duration-as-reduction)
gives the Olympics its appeal as spectacle, but it is the
temporality of the Olympiad (duration-as-continuity) that
provides its appeal as ideology. Thus, in the play of
signification so essential to the Olympics, the one symbol that
stands unique from the rest is the Olympic Torch, signifier of
continuity and simulacrum of an eternal flame that reaches
back to Antiquity as if Prometheus himself delivered us a
gesture of hope in the decorative wrap of athletic progress.

.043 Torch as Microarchitecture

...the Olympic Torch also offers a host nation unique opportunities to transgress the sovereign boundaries of the local via the Olympic Torch Relay. Duration-as-continuity merges with the flows and disconnects of global capital in creating new messages to coexist with those imagined to have existed for thousands of years. It is here that Virilio offers a clue to the question posed earlier by Baudrillard: "History as the extensiveness of time—of time that lasts, is portioned out, organized, developed—is disappearing in favour of the instant, as if the end of history were the end of duration in favour of instantaneousness, and of course, of ubiquity." If space-as-extension was destroyed on 9/11, a semiotic raising of the stakes for terrorism suggests that time-as-duration must be next: it is this simulacrum of an eternal flame that must be violently destroyed.

.051 Superhumans and Mutants

The light speed of the nuclear blasts in Hiroshima and Nagasaki forced a recalibration of other speeds as well. The Cold War that succeeded these two detonations witnessed one such recalibration: while proxy wars were fought in the jungles of the underdeveloped world, they were contested in the sporting arenas of the overdeveloped world as well. East versus West sporting competition in the name of ideology launched a total rationalization of the athletic body as an object of science that could be engineered for the optimal pursuit of speed. The fallout from this proxy sporting war was most notably observed in the national sports teams of East Germany, which implemented programs of anabolic steroid use for both its male and female athletes, resulting in short-term athletic success at the expense of substantial physical deformities later in life. From state-sponsored subhumanization to state-sponsored superhumanization and its mutant consequences in a matter of three decades, the jackboot march of progress...

.052 Organic and Machinic Vision

...describing the organic vision of an individual human subject, Brian Massumi observes that there can be no sight without the faculties of tactility and movement. Virilio similarly recognizes in the context of machinic vision that technical optics have become kinematic and that the perception of touch has become integral to such a vision. The technical apparatus leveraged by the moebius band of surveillance and spectacle emerges due to the incapability of organic vision to administer bodies and preserve the integrity of the enclosure at high speeds or broad spatial scales. We might suggest that the social abstraction, ordering, and processing demanded of a machinic visual faculty is not possible without the tactile enabling of the digital pulses of electrical information that constitute its technical apparatus. And while movement is required for this machinic form of sensation to become possible, since the technical apparatus is normally fixed in space, the relationship is inverted such that movement is required of the objects themselves.

.053 Critical Space

Doping has persisted beyond this earlier acceleration during the Cold War to become today a free market network of individual athletes, coaches and scientists who push the biochemical and physiological limits of the body in competition. Meanwhile, the same technological infrastructure that enabled a stable communications network in case of a nuclear attack is leveraged by the World Anti-Doping Agency for the global surveillance of world-class high performance athletes. The nuclear bomb is to deterrence as the information bomb is to the control society...

.054 Filial to File

...film-based photography of Walter Benjamin's era, the technical apparatus required light-sensitive chemical reactions to take place in order for the original image to be reproduced in its negative state. To create a positive print from this negative one would further submit the film and photographic paper to specific chemical processes, inverting the colours and spatial coordinates in the process. To continue producing copies of the image—that is, to move from the chemical to the mechanical reproductions of which Benjamin analyzed—always requires a return to the original negative print. This bond is obsolesced in the age of the digital, when file replaces the filial. Every digital image contains within it all of the information required to make a perfect copy of itself, not for mechanical reproduction, but for digital replication. If the cameraman was a surgeon to the painter's magician in Benjamin's analysis, then the digital photographer is a geneticist who creates new memes and replicates them throughout the network.

.061 Two Information Bombs

Given the historical difficulties encountered in attempting to weaponize the biological, as outlined by Critical Art Ensemble, we do not have an authoritative example of the genetic or biological bomb in its weaponized form. But understanding that the genetic is in the domain of code suggests that we might peruse the realm of information for clues. Consider the notorious ILOVEYOU computer virus, a worm spread throughout the internet by the contagion vector of forwarded email in May 2000. It suggests that if we are to consider the bomb in its traditional sense of intentionality then we may speak of a second catastrophic bomb of the information sort: one of viral contagion to complement that of the nuclear blast...

.062 Simulated Sexuality

...the nexus of technology, sex and play, the Olympics and its collection of sleek, muscular and nubile bodies is billed as an exclusive VIP club in which those without a chance to win or who have already been eliminated from competition engage in carnal forms of bacchanalia. 130,000 condoms were given out to open the 2004 Athens Games, the largest Trojan onslaught there since Antiquity, and the 2008 Beijing Games offered more of the same. Prophylactic layer intact, our sporting deities engage in their festivities within the ever-shifting nomadism of the athlete's village, while the global village congregation of spectators experiences the Olympic mythos and its simulated sex as a release of the tensile bondage between libidinal and lipidinal—via the digital prophylactic of the screenal economy.

.063 Breaker vs. Filter

...converting the nuclear from weapon to property form we introduce the *breaker* as the safety device that prevents the accident becoming manifest from its potential. That is, the device that interrupts the flow is one of binary logic, either on or off. The flows of the genetic and the memetic proceed on an altogether different basis. One difficulty in weaponizing the biological involves heat: the detonation of a biological weapon can be of sufficiently high temperature that it kills all virulent material within. In her articulation of the informatics of domination, however, Donna Haraway notes that heat yields to noise, which suggests an altogether different problem for weaponization. Genes and memes cannot be enclosed in the same fashion as the nuclear and, as such, the breaker is replaced by the *filter*, the statistical model that surfs the wave between signal and noise.

.064 Contagion and Diaspora

...to the ILOVEYOU virus, its vectors of contagion were not simply random or even contained within a local geography, but were rather based on the affinity networks linked by email address books representing a wide variety of identities ranging from the filial to the corporate to the ludic. While ILOVEYOU was at any time able to move rhizomatically from one point to another across the network, as a matter of probability it more often stayed within the particular flows of subjectivity that characterized the lived everyday of any particular host. That said, these flows and their composition are always themselves contingent and in flux, which suggests that the detonation of the genetic bomb will not occur locally (as with Little Boy and Fat Man) nor globally (as with 9/11), but rather *diasporally*.

.071 Body Doubling

In television and film, the *stand-in* allows the director to block the performance of a scene by setting camera angles and adjusting lighting with bodies of the approximate size that will be used during filming. The stand-in's performance occurs entirely before shooting takes place; that is, the stand-in never actually appears on camera and is only incidentally integral to the final product. We might contrast the stand-in with the *body double*, who actually appears on film as a replacement for the star talent in dangerous "stunt" situations, to provide some particular skill that the star actor is missing, or as a surrogate for sexual situations involving nudity. The performance of the double is key to the final production though it is usually realized anonymously: while generic credit is given for double work, very rarely is there specific acknowledgment for a particular scene delivered...

.072 Under Pressure

If Virilio asks us to consider a logic and politics of speed, does it not follow that we are to consider a logic and politics of pressure as well? If the particles within any closed volumetric system accelerate to higher speeds, they collide more frequently with greater momentum and increase the pressure within that closed system. (More collisions, more tactile relations, more potential for contagion.) That is, unless there is some exogenous temperature coolant to offset the increases in the other thermodynamic variables. But if light speed signals a final enclosure of the planet and the particles within continue to accelerate (bodies, vehicles, data, capital), then whence the coolant? We might suggest that the coolant appears to be, at least for the time being, the controlled foldings of virtual ludic space...

.073 Body Trebling

...interactive videogames the relationship changes once again. In the production of many sports titles we have relatively cheap and anonymous "talent" acting as body doubles for the celebrity athletes who appear in the game. The performance of the double is key to the final production of the game: the points of light recorded in a motion capture session create generic construct skeletons to which celebrity flesh is texture-mapped at a later time. Film (pellicule) as the substrate of celluloid reproduction has yielded to skin (pellicule) as the object of celebrity replication. We still do not have a final performance, however. Though the construct possesses a skeleton (via motion capture), musculature (via programmed algorithms) and flesh (via photos/video/facial scans), it lacks the central nervous system with which it performs. It is the "user"—or the *body treble*—that brings the construct to life and animates the final performance. In these topological spaces of athletic body and ludic arena lie the dendrites of social control, but also the potential...

.081 Inversion: Torch as Weapon

...February 2006 emails began to appear warning of an "Olympic Torch" virus that was embedded in messages bearing the subject line "Invitation" and would erase the hard disk of the user's computer when opened. But the "Olympic Torch" virus was a hoax. The purported virus did not actually exist, though since the warning email reported an acknowledgement of its veracity by such reputable sources as CNN, McAfee and Microsoft, many recipients forwarded the warning so contacts could take the necessary precautions. Bypassing filters through networks of trust: inoculations against the weapon are also implicated in the accident, *proactivity* the third form of pollution to join radioactivity and interactivity.

.082 Weapon: Torch as Inversion

...memes raged out of control along the Olympic Torch relay route. In support of Tibetan independence from Chinese rule, the symptoms of protest emerged in London, Paris, San Francisco and elsewhere. Metonymically representing Beijing's authority in Tibet, the torch was extinguished during the protests, not once but twice. Though it was re-lit each time, the continuity was broken. Organizers suggested aborting the Canberra leg of the global relay, where contagion was already beginning to foment. "I think that would be tantamount to giving in to terrorism," replied Australian Olympic Committee president John Coates.

.083 He Kexin

...physics of world class gymnastics are such that only those bodies maximizing the calculus between strength and malleability are capable of reaching the highest of performance levels today. Since this has meant increasingly younger athletes in the folds of competition, the Fédération Internationale de Gymnastique stipulates a minimum age of 16 years for Olympic competition. But rumours began to surface that the Chinese gymnast He Kexin, a gold medal favourite, was competing underage. Chinese officials denied the allegations, citing He's passport as proof of age. By combing English and Chinese search engines, a computer security expert known as "Stryde" was able to find copies of old registration documents that suggested He was indeed underage. "Stryde" made the findings public, after which the files in question began to disappear from the original Chinese servers. But in their indexing to search engines, these files were replicated to a caching system, forensic traces that allowed "Stryde" to further replicate the files and publish them. Others following the story themselves began to make screen captures of the files in question showing the timestamp from the archive, and the "evidence" was quickly replicated throughout a multitudinous swarm.

.084 He Kexin

...dynamic between the cleansing of the archive by those in control and the temporality of the traces in the cache that were captured and replicated by many in opposition is of significant interest. If, as Marshall McLuhan suggested, truth becomes trust in the age of electric communications, then who can we trust? The powerful institutions of modernity are being challenged by a multitudinous swarm that takes forensic traces from the archive and replicates them across the network to create its own critical mass of trust. How are the ethics and biases of this networked organic entity either resolved or dissolved? It is worth noting that many of these screen captures taken by virtual cameras are themselves not text-searchable by the major search engines. Hence, the filename of the image or the hyperlink back to the original *Stryde Hax* blog post reintroduces a filial relation to the communication.

Or, perhaps it metastasizes to form its own excess of self-referentiality.

.085 He Kexin

From the singularity of 9/11 to the multiplicity of signs and their mutations that constituted the Beijing Olympic Games to the multitude that sought to contest a theretofore hegemonic truth. Two information bombs, one nuclear and one genetic, one primarily optic and the other primarily haptic. Where does the political take up from these new aesthetics? It is no longer simply a matter of tracing property forms and lines of ownership, nor a matter of developing a weapon to continue the political by other means. Can politics be resurrected in the liminality between the embodied everyday and the fractalization of space made possible by the camera and screen? If the contemporary condition of our grey ecology is marked by the finitude of extensive planetary space, the pollution of our lived distances by real-time transmission, and the temporary reprieve offered by the foldings and tremblings of the data-virtual, we can ask no less of a question today.

Works Cited

Associated Press, "IOC to Review Beijing Torch Problems, Upcoming International Relays" AOL Sports India.

http://www.aol.in/sports/story/200804081411003062056S/2090/index.html (April 8, 2008)

J. Baudrillard, *The Spirit of Terrorism* trans. Chris Turner (London: Verso, 2002)

R. Beamish and I. Ritchie, *Fastest, Highest, Strongest: A Critique of High-Performance Sport* (New York: Routledge, 2006)

W. Benjamin, "The Work of Art in the Age of Mechanical Reproduction." *Illuminations: Essays and Reflections* (pp. 217-252) trans. H Zohn (New York: Schocken, 1968)

Critical Art Ensemble, *Marching Plague: Germ Warfare and Global Public Health* (New York: Autonomedia, 2006)

G. Deleuze and F. Guattari, *A Thousand Plateaus: Capitalism and Schizophrenia* trans. Brian Massumi (Minnesota: University of Minnesota Press, 1987)

D. Haraway, *Simians, Cyborgs, and Women: The Reinvention of Nature* (Oxford: Taylor & Francis, 1990)

B. Massumi, *Parables for the Virtual: Movement, Affect, Sensation* (Durham, NC: Duke University Press, 2002)

M. McLuhan, *Understanding Media: The Extensions of Man* (Toronto: Signet, 1964)

Complexity in the Age of Simplicity

Michael Hirsch

A major subfield in the philosophy of science examines the
process of theory development and change. In approaching a
problem, scientists often employ reductionistic research
strategies, including those of decomposition and localization,
to develop mechanistic explanations of scientific phenomena.
Such strategies rest upon the assumption that the behavior of a
system can be accounted for in terms of the functions
performed by its component parts and the interactions between
those parts. Philosophers of science note, however, that
scientific problems are often ill defined: William Bechtel and
Robert Richardson assert, "The constraints defining an
adequate solution are not sharply delineated, and even the
structure of the problem space itself is unclear" (*Discovering
Complexity,* 15). Identifying the appropriate level of analysis
– the problem space, unit of selection or locus of control – is
the first step in experimentation. Should the scientist
mistakenly determine a level that is either too high (too all-
encompassing, and so, not taking into account the interaction
of components in the behavior of the system) or too low
(overly reliant on direct localization, which ultimately tells
only *what* component or set of components is causing a given
effect, not *how* the effect is produced), the unfolding of the
research project is doomed to failure. Failure is not to be
understood only in its negative connotation; as this paper will
show, failures can sometimes be as revealing as successes.
Nevertheless, the terms according to which a problem is
framed from the outset govern the character of theories which
emerge later on. These theories, in turn, shape the direction of
future research programs that drive scientific change.

Ideological commitments and social contexts influence and,
oftentimes, interfere with scientific determinations. French
philosopher and self-described "art critic of technologies,"
Paul Virilio, has characterized our present experience of living
in a world bombarded by rapid techno-scientific development
in terms of what he calls the military-industrial technosphere.

Virilio's writing succeeds in being not only diagnostic, but invitational: often wrongly conceived as pessimistic, negative and apocalyptic, Virilio's writing is better understood as a call to action. In particular, Virilio calls us to conduct a more rigorous critique of media and technology in relation to their effect upon the human condition. Many thinkers have taken up Virilio's call to critique such things as bio-medical prostheses, military-cinematic 'intelligence' systems, and telecommunicational gadgets, as well as the effects these technologies have on individuals and society. Yet philosophers have thus far abstained from taking Virilio's call to a deeper level, namely to that of the very nature of the thought processes which inform and propel techno-scientific development. If, as Virilio suggests, our present reality is characterized by a disturbance in the perception of what reality is in the first place – a phenomenon he refers to as dromospheric pollution – then the basic assumptions of scientific discovery may no longer hold and the fundamental impulse for techno-scientific development may be both eluding and deluding us. It is, therefore, no accident that Virilio's work has concentrated on uncovering the logic and impact of speed on the human condition, speed made manifest in teletechnologies and telecommunications.

Rather than focusing on the distinction Virilio makes between relative and absolute speed, and rather than addressing the political impact Virilio assigns to dromology, I will entertain an aspect of Virilio's thoughts on speed that have been un(der)acknowledged. Speed, as I will argue in this essay, is problematic insofar as it is leading to ever greater complexity, which in turn is enabling systems to operate at an ever faster speed. This very idea is, of course, somewhat unexpected and paradoxical. The logic of complexity is such that the more complex a problem is, the more time it takes me to complete it: hence, increased complexity implies decreased speed. Yet, the world Virilio describes – a description in general that I find both empirically and phenomenologically valid – is a world that seems to speed up despite the complex systems required to support such a dromological infrastructure. Speed, it seems, is complexity masquerading as simplicity. It seems so simple to watch live gymnastics in Beijing on Comcast from my home in Massachusetts, USA; to Skype my friends in Prague with a live video feed; to Gmail a message to a distribution list of 1000. Yet each of these rather mundane activities is driven by sophisticated technological and scientific processes – processes that are both invisible and incomprehensible to the average user.

Which is why Virilio is so important to us today: Virilio's critical method helps to make the invisible visible; in other words, Virilio teaches us to look beyond and beneath the façade of scientific progress for the mechanisms of power and control that alter our perception of reality. I shall argue, therefore, that Virilio's greatest contribution to contemporary debates about "globalization," telecommunications, and military science, is the very thought process by which he approaches these issues. In writing *about* Virilio, I shall attempt to reveal the important ways he teaches us to think about science and technology in terms of modification and change. Accordingly, I shall demonstrate that Virilio's theory of dromology serves as an important heuristical constraint on scientific research practices: research strategies which employ the heuristic of speed will help philosophers of media and communications, as well as philosophers of science and technology to think more rigorously about the systems, networks and invisible architecture that comprise our present 'virtual' predicament. If, as Virilio maintains, we should "add to the concerns of *green ecology* those of a *grey ecology* that would focus on the postindustrial degradation of the depth of field of the terrestrial landscape" (*Open Sky*, 41), it is imperative for thinkers to understand and critique the methodology driving techno-scientific development in the 21st-century.

Machine Worship

In an interview with David Dufresne for the Après-Coup Psychoanalytic Association, Paul Virilio asserts, "When machines begin to be idolized, social catastrophe is never far behind" ("Cyberesistance Fighter"). Virilio's remark underscores a central tenet of his thought, namely that when it comes to techno-scientific development successes and failures are deceptively ambivalent. While on the one hand scientific progress has made tremendous improvements in such important public sectors as pharmacology, transportation and communications, there is a consequence – what Virilio refers to as 'the failure of the success of progress.' Media, particularly in the form of advertisements and pop culture, tends to inflate the successful or positive aspects of development, while deflating or even censoring altogether what Virilio calls 'the accident:' in *Open Sky*, for instance, Virilio writes, "Unless we are deliberately forgetting *the invention of the shipwreck* in the invention of the ship or *the rail accident* in the advent of the train, we need to examine the hidden face of new technologies, before that face reveals itself in spite of us" (40). Although the accident – the inherent potential for derailment – is intentionally much less visible than the ostensible benefits of any given development, this 'hidden face' deserves critical attention.

When machines begin to be idolized, apotheosis has occurred. Accordingly, the concept *deus ex machina* becomes simply *machina deus:* the machine is no longer a vehicle through which a god appears or is revealed, but rather the machine *is* god, the machine incarnates god, hypostasizes god. Far from simply rendering the God-of-our-fathers impotent or redundant as has often been supposed, techno-scientific development as manifest in the machine *actually becomes* God, deposing the Judeo-Christian-Islamic God with a more relevant successor. This new god, the machine-god, displays certain characteristics, which at times betray the accident of this divine transformation.

To the Latin ear, we should remember, *machina* would generally suggest a siege-engine, hence, a war machine. This connection becomes all the more important when we consider Virilio's abundant work on the military-industrial complex. In *Speed and Politics*, for instance, Virilio makes one of his most succinct statements about the triumvirate of war, dromology and the human predicament: "We have to face the facts: today, speed is war, the last war" (139). The force of this reproach comes from Virilio's concern that we, in fact, are not facing the facts, that we are filtering away the reality of the accident from our comprehensive awareness of techno-scientific development. According to Virilio, it is precisely through the technological and industrial development of weaponry – again, of the war machine – that speed has become war. (It is also important to note that since the publication of *Speed and Politics* in 1977, Virilio has himself 'faced the facts' insofar as war no longer means only 'war *of* the world' – combat between more or less sovereign entities – but also 'war *on* the world' as demonstrated by his call for a grey ecology.) In a Ctheory interview with John Armitage, Virilio avers, "nowadays, the tragedy of war is mediated through technology. It is no longer mediated through the human being with moral responsibilities. It is mediated through the destructive power of the atomic bomb." Our absolute faith in *machina deus* confers upon the machine the power to make decisions, control behavior and plan strategies. While machines orchestrate and perform war (including ecological war), the human is side-lined, made both a spectator and consumer of war images and war destruction.

In addition to the bellicose connotation, 'engine of war,' *machina* also carries the sense of device, trick or contrivance, much like that which one hears in the English derivative, 'machination.' This meaning is etymologically germane to the theater, where the term 'machinery' originally referred to the mechanical devices used for creating special effects on the performance stage. Like an intricate *mise en scene* intended to lure the audience into a make-believe world, machines trick us into thinking something other than that which is the case. For example, machines trick us into thinking that complexity is simplicity – this, of course, is the ingenuity of Windows operating systems, an operational complexity rendered still more 'simple' in the user interface of Apple computers. In a word, the 'work' of machinery is the deception of perception. Virilio's observation that our very perception is under attack in the dromosphere points to this aspect of machinery's chicanery. In *War and Cinema* he writes,

"[News footage] isn't really news footage any longer, but the *raw material of vision*, the most trustworthy kind possible. The extraordinary commercialization of audiovisual technology is responding to the same demand. For videos and walkmans are reality and appearance in kit form: we use them not to watch films or listen to music, but to add vision and soundtracks, to make us directors of our own reality." (66)

Hence, it is not only that the machine itself often masquerades as something that it is not (robots that look like humans, player-pianos, two-way mirrors, wall-mounted flat-screen TVs that play one long still-shot of famous artwork), but also that the machine disrupts and disturbs our very perception of reality. Virilio explains, "Perceived reality is being split into the real and the virtual, and we are getting a kind of stereoreality, in which existence loses its reference points…But cyberspace and instantaneous, globalized information are throwing [existence] into confusion. What is now underway is a disturbance of the perception of the real: a trauma" ("Red Alert in Cyberspace!"). The strategic power of deception brandished by the *machina deus* dupes us into embracing a cycle of self-imposed trauma: the machine – which, with Dr. Frankenstein we must remember is always a product of our own creation – makes us think we are being graciously served when we are really being secretly traumatized (in fact, it creates an environment in which the thought of traumatization would never – *could never* – occur) and, despite the damage being done to ourselves, it makes us want more, more, more.

The *machina deus*, in sum, is machine-god, Mars-machine and con-god all in one. The apotheosis of the machine suggests a change in ontic status from a mechanical apparatus into something else, something Other, something transcendentally material. The *accident* of the machine, we could say, is the machine-god: in the creation of the machine is the creation of the machine-god, which consequently reveals the *substitution* of the transcendental God. Another way of saying this is that in its *virtual* machine form, the *real* (original, transcendental) G/god *becomes more real*. Virtuality effaces the very hiddenness of G/god, rendering absence presence, and thereby establishing G/godself in the real space of the machine. Contra Jean Baudrillard's notion of simulation, Virilio prefers the language of substitution: "I don't believe in simulationism...As I see it, new technologies are substituting a virtual reality for an actual reality. And this is more than a phase: it's a definite change" ("Cyberwar, God and Television"). Hence, to denominate the ontogenetical deification of machines, let us aver that the virtual has *substituted* for the real, thereby assuming the real – ontologically and phenomenologically – in its stead. In theological terms, the phenomenon of machine worship can be captured in the mock creedal formula, "We believe in the Virtual, because the Virtual is the Real Real."

Such a creed, preposterous as it is, nevertheless says as much about those who could hypothetically utter it as it does about the Being to whom it refers. Virilio's remark to Dufresne, after all, concerns not only machines but also those who worship them: "social catastrophe," we must remember, "is never far behind." Idolatry operates not only on a transcendental-religious plane, but also affects inter-human relations: idolatry involves the relationship between humans and god(s) via the mediation of a made object. If religion has taught us anything it is that the relationship between humans and god(s) is furthermore reflected in the relationship between humans to each other. When our god reveals itself to be a machine-god, a Mars-god and a con-god, the *imitatio dei* becomes a suicidal call for worldwide annihilation. Hence, when machines begin to be idolized, it bespeaks the frightening truth that techno-scientific developments have fundamentally challenged what it means to be human.

The Structure of Scientific Success Stories (and their failures)

Such a dystopic vision of an Orwellian machine-religion may help us gain a deeper understanding of the failure of the success of techno-scientific progress. Virilio helps us see that the very successes lauded by technophiles, infonauts and operational scientists often veil the truth of catastrophic failure. Specifically, Virilio refers to this failure as dromospheric pollution, the postindustrial pollution to which his call for a grey ecology responds. Of dromospheric pollution, Virilio writes:

"Contamination has in fact spread further than the elements, natural substances, air, water, flora and fauna it attacks – as far as the space-time of our planet. Gradually reduced to nothing by the various tools of transport and instantaneous communication, the geophysical environment is undergoing an alarming diminishing of its 'depth of field' and this is degrading man's relationship with his environment" (*Open Sky*, 22).

Dromospheric pollution, in other words, contaminates our very sense of space and place, earth and world. But it is more than the erosion of the geophysical environment that is at stake – dromospheric pollution eats away at the social fabric that undergirds human communities. Although technologies like Skype, Facebook and Instant Messenger make us feel like we are more connected with our neighbors, the truth is that we are more disconnected than ever. Moreover, this disconnection is not simply a rupture between one and the other: my personal lack of any real, meaningful contact with others presages my ultimate extrication from myself. In the dromosphere, my avatar becomes the real me. Dromospheric pollution reduces the subject to a virtual substitution of itself.

Despite this rather grim assessment of life in the dromosphere, Virilio, it must be stressed, is by no means an out-and-out foe of technology and scientific discovery. Rather, the persistent theme running throughout his many writings and interviews, is that "only if one is guarded against its dangers will it be possible to enjoy the positive aspects of the developments in the realm of new technologies" ("Global Algorithm 1.7"). Grey ecology signals a caution, a warning, a red alert that techno-scientific development cannot proceed *unchecked*. There are, most certainly, aspects of development that deserve praise and thanksgiving, aspects which bring greater comfort, better health, increased productivity. Yet, the *pro*gress of machines simply cannot continue to pro*gress* with such growing speed; if it does, we face the very real possibility that machines will so radically alter our perception of reality, ultimately blinding us to what it means to be human. Increased productivity, for instance, can quickly lead to increased subjectivity – specifically, increased subjectivity to productivity – whereby we literally become slaves to the machine.

Underscoring the need for a grey ecology, Virilio correspondingly calls for techno-scientific development *with critique*. The challenges for us living in the dromosphere, where the rule of speed propels development ever-onwards, are twofold: discovery is outrunning theory, and the culture of development continuously overstates its successes in the popular media while the possibility of a complete, architectonic collapse of the postindustrial complex is denied. Accordingly, two complaints against the culture of development emerge: for one, progress in the realm of techno-scientific development should never go unqualified; and secondly, development in the 21st-century is lacking theoretical support to interpret, justify and evaluate the unprecedented speed of invention and manufacturing. Both complaints, I believe, are at the center of Virilio's thought.

But, both complaints also push Virilio's thought to a deeper level of analysis: it is not enough to critique new technologies after they have already been introduced; our critique must occur at the level of the thought processes which drive techno-scientific modification and change in the first place.

To begin, Virilio's thought calls into question a for-granted assumption about the nature of progress. In our common vernacular, progress is too often equated unequivocally with the good. This in itself should signal a failure of progress' success. When progress becomes the goal of research, industry and science, it is easy to lose sight of the effects, outcomes and consequences along the way. 'State-of-the-art' comes to refer more to the technique or process of development than the tangible product. For example, a so-called state-of-the-art video recorder suggests a device which is easier to use, less cumbersome, and offers more features in a single unit than earlier models; state-of-the-art, therefore, would seem to refer to a general simplification regarding the mechanical explanation of the thing itself. Yet, this is anything but the case. While the latest device is simpler and more mundane than ever (my phone, timepiece, camera, video recorder, stereo, video game machine, library, GPS, and Wi-Fi are all included in one single 2x3 inch razor-thin piece of plastic), what is state-of-the-art are the complex technical processes enabling the new gadget. These processes and techniques remain utterly invisible and inaccessible to the vast majority of us.

The epistemic concern is not that the average consumer needs to know how her digital camera 'works' mechanically, but that the opacity of techno-scientific processes and techniques eclipses what Virilio calls 'the accident.' Because we forget – albeit this is largely an *accidental* forgetting (in the common sense of the term) on account of the fact that that which we have forgotten was never made apparent to us from the outset – that "to invent something is to invent the accident," we now find ourselves ill-equipped to respond to potential derailment, to the negative, dangerous side of techno-scientific development. In truth, we are ill-equipped to respond to the failure of progress:

"To invent something is to invent the accident. To invent the ship is to invent the shipwreck; the space shuttle, the explosion. And to invent the electronic superhighway or the Internet is to invent a major risk which is not easily spotted because it does not produce fatalities like a shipwreck or a mid-air explosion. The information accident is, sadly, not very visible. It is immaterial like the waves that carry information." ("Cyberesistance Fighter").

Unless we are at least minimally aware of the accident upon its invention, we will not be able to prepare ourselves for either a technological disaster like that which occurred on January 28, 1986 when the Space Shuttle *Challenger* exploded just 73 seconds after launch, let alone an informational disaster of unconscionable proportions like that predicted by Virilio. And, so long as we continue to inhabit the dromosphere, where the twin phenomena of immediacy and instantaneity reign supreme, the invisible, immaterial expression of the accident is likely to occur without our even knowing it, long before it is too late. Despite the expectations of the United States Department of Homeland Security, it is all too likely that the next global, cataclysmic disaster will be launched not in the name of Allah, but in the name of techno-scientific progress.

In addition to the call to keep a critical eye on the celebrated accomplishments of progress, Virilio's writings argue for a sort of re-engineering of philosophy, for new critical perspectives on how to make sense of emerging techno-scientific complexities. We can see the beginnings of a new theoretical approach in Virilio's coinage of words stemming from the Greek word *dromos*, meaning 'a race' or 'running': "In fact, there was no 'industrial revolution,' but only a 'dromocratic revolution'; there is no democracy, only dromocracy; there is no strategy, only dromology" (*Speed and Politics*, 46). Virilio's idea of dromology has been helpful in conducting thoughtful critiques of science and technology from the perspective of politics, aesthetics, and, to a somewhat lesser extent, ethics. I believe dromology can go further still. Dromology is able to work against the rigidly deductive-nomological rationalizations of traditional apodeictic (scientific) language. I suggest, therefore, that dromology may be useful to philosophers of science and technology, who seek to understand and evaluate the latest developments in scientific theory and praxis.

Techniques and procedures, together with the explanatory account scientists give for causal factors and mechanistic models of system behavior, may reveal the sort of information about the accident – about the untold story of technology's negative side – that Virilio claims is lacking from our current understanding. If we are able to identify a grain of hope in Virilio's thought, it is that the more information we are able to glean about the invention of the accident, the more likely it will be for humanity to save itself from the threat of absolute virtuality. Our critical/theoretical/philosophical task is not easy. Dromospheric pollution obfuscates the analytical landscape, "shattering *man's unity of perception* and...producing, this time AUTOMATICALLY, the persistence of a disturbance in self-perception that will have lasting effects on man's rapport with the real" (*The Art of the Motor*, 147). In order to overcome the apparent obstacles posed by dromology, philosophers of science and technology must use dromology to their advantage, waging a theoretical fight-fire-with-fire counter-insurgency of speed-against-speed. Similar to excitatory methods of research, where scientists impose an unusually strong stimulus into a system in order to elicit an unambiguous response, thereby allowing them to predict and interpret system behavior more accurately, dromology can function as an heuristic aid to help us evaluate complex systems that are already operating at an unprecedented rate of speed.

The history of scientific discovery reveals that the solutions of one generation are often the very problems of the next.

Problem solving is, in other words, dynamic. In tracing and evaluating scientific discovery, philosophers of science and technology are principally concerned with the kinematics of change. Science, of course, is a much more precarious and developmental endeavor than the popular media would lead us to believe. Scientific discovery is often approximate; scientists often encounter unpredictable causal chains; systems often operate according to nonlinear, irregular patterns of behavior; historical contingencies, cognitive strategies, environmental conditions and technical resources all have an effect on scientific theory and praxis. The challenge facing the contemporary techno-scientific enterprise is that, under the influence of dromology, all of these quasi-secret characteristics of scientific modification and change are exacerbated. In short, techno-scientific development is growing increasingly complex, and changes are occurring more rapidly and suddenly than ever before. Yet most of this complexity and most of these changes remain unseen by the average consumer. Indeed, the tendency towards complexification is in sharp contrast to our day-to-day, hands-on experience of these developments: outpatient laser surgeries, Verizon Wireless and robotic vacuum cleaners all point instead to effortlessness, comfort and simplicity. Truly, the signature of our epoch is complexity masquerading as simplicity.

Yet it is complexity, as well as the troubling paradox that greater complexity continues to yield ever faster rates of processing and operation, that should give us pause. As we have seen, when we lose sight of the forces at play within our world, the society of success quickly converts into the society of control. Complex systems – invisible, impenetrable and impervious to our understanding – come to control our thoughts, decisions and actions. Such complexity presents considerable difficulty to the scientific analyst or philosopher. Bechtel and Richardson observe:

"Recent research in the psychology of judgment indicates that humans have great difficulty comprehending cases with more than a few interacting variables. Humans *cannot* use information involving large numbers of components or complex interactions of components, and even when the problem tasks are computationally tractable, human beings *do not* approach them in this way. Complex systems are computationally as well as psychologically unmanageable for humans" (*Discovering Complexity*, 27).

This cognitive limitation may explain one reason why complexity is so often able to masquerade as simplicity – it simply has to. We humans would shut down in the face of a network model that is too complex: nonlinear, integrated, multi-connectional, non-decomposable systems overwhelm our capacity for understanding. Nevertheless, these are precisely the systems with which we are faced at the dawn of a new millennium.

It is hard to know how to approach such systems. We cannot sit passively by, while technologies grow ever more complex, especially not *by their own making*. We have already explored the consequences when machines begin to be idolized; the next step, when machines take on a life of their own, when machines advance from being machine-gods to becoming creator-gods, capable of inventing technologies incomprehensible to human cognition, will signal a true social catastrophe of imponderable magnitude. In order to best address the phenomena of complex systems, it is optimal for researchers to employ heuristic strategies. This, in and of itself, is nothing new: decomposition and localization are heuristics frequently utilized by scientists when embarking upon an explanatory task. Heuristics such as these can help researchers limit their search space, in turn simplifying the problems posed. Bechtel and Richardson highlight an interesting characteristic of heuristics: "heuristics are strategies prone to failure. It is precisely where heuristics fail that their role in the development of science is the clearest" (ibid. 37). The failure of heuristics often leads to the discovery of additional important influences on system behavior. This tendency toward failure is, perhaps somewhat surprisingly, key to scientific discovery, modification and change. My suggestion, however, is that the simplifying tendency of heuristics – simplification that results in systematic failure – is potentially misleading. Simplicity, we recall, has been leading us astray; complexity masquerading as simplicity blinds us to the accident.

Building off the thought and methodology of Paul Virilio, I suggest that that we consider dromology as an heuristical constraint on scientific research practices. Rather than aiming towards simplification of the explanatory task, a dromological approach would aim towards complexification. Further complexifying already complex systems will likely lead to a similar systematic failure as when heuristics are employed to simplify causal networks. Complexification, however, will shed additional light on the complexity of the integrated component systems with which we are faced today. Dromology as an heuristical constraint involves speeding up already hyper systems. The goal of such a procedure is to overexcite a system to the point of failure. Excitation will trigger the accident *under laboratory controls*. Dromological research strategies, therefore, will reveal the threshold capacity of the system, as well as the nature and identity of the accident in question. The more we know about the accident, the better equipped we will be as a society to respond to future disasters.

Because complexity masquerades as simplicity, new perspectives on research in the philosophy of science and technology should aim to unmask complex systems. Virilio's call for a grey ecology aims not only to help us avoid disaster in the name of progress. When applied to scientific research strategies, the pursuit of a grey ecology first and foremost helps us identify the disaster itself – the accident waiting to happen. It is, after all, one thing to be afraid, something wholly other to not know what one is afraid of.

Works Cited

W. Bechtel and R. Richardson, *Discovering Complexity: Decomposition and Localization As Strategies in Scientific Research* (Princeton: Princeton University Press, 1993)

P.Virilio, *The Art of the Motor* trans. Julie Rose (Minneapolis: University of Minnesota Press, 1995)

P. Virilio, *Open Sky* trans. Julie Rose (London: Verso, 1997)

P. Virilio, "Red Alert in Cyberspace!" found on *Radical Philosophy* Nov/Dec 1995, www.radicalphilosophy.com/default.asp?channel_id=2187&editorial_id=10735

P. Virilio, *Speed and Politics: An Essay on Dromology* (New York: Semiotext(e), 1977/1986)

P. Virilio, *War and Cinema: The Logistics of Perception* trans. P. Camilier (London: Verso, 1984/1989)

P. Virilio and J. Armitage, "Ctheory Interview with Paul Virilio: The Kosovo War Took Place In Orbital Space," 10/18/2000, www.ctheory.net/articles.aspx?id=132

P. Virilio and D. Dufresne, "Cyberesistance Fighter – An Interview with Paul Virilio," www.apres-coup.org/mt/archives/title/2005/01/cyberesistance.html

P. Virilio and C. Oliveira, "Global Algorithm 1.7: The Silence of the Lambs: Paul Virilio in Conversation," 06/12/1996, www.ctheory.net/articles.aspx?id=38

P.Virilio and L. Wilson, "Cyberwar, God and Television: Interview with Paul Virilio," 12/01/1994, www.ctheory.net/articles.aspx?id=62

Crash: Ballard, Virilio, Bataille

Daniel Brittain

J.G. Ballard's *Crash* is about auto accidents. The main character Ballard accidentally drives into oncoming traffic crashing into a car moving Mr. and Mrs. Remington. Killing Mr. Remington, Ballard survives and in the hospital meets Vaughn, a ringleader of accident survivors charged by near death experience. Vaughn envisions accidents, leading to his own death trying to penetrate Elizabeth Taylor by driving his car off an Airport Overpass onto her vehicle.

Crash's fixation on airport landscapes, characters' perverse sexual and physical life styles and car crashes provides a Story for exploring contemporary life. Contemporary life dominated by transportation with an increasingly burdensome emphasis placed upon the perpetual finding of energy to enable transportation. Playing with elements from *Crash*, this essay deconstructs the Story using the character Vaughn, the landscape of the airport and access roads, the auto industry's simulated accident, and the recreation of a spectacular auto-accident. Beginning with reading Vaughn as the new dromoscopic citizen, the deconstruction then studies the World and its possible becoming through directed expenditure and logistics. Using the space and speed that is opened in the World by the interaction of expenditure and logistics, the deconstruction returns to a study of Character, finding an origin of Character founded upon violence, and that because of the foundation on violence, the necessary creation of a cult towards violence, that, like Borges's sexual *Sect of the Phoenix*, all participate in.

Stuck with Vaughn

The traffic jam, paradox of the trip, bane of transportation, break. The experience imagined: rush hour, an accident, rubber necking, bottle necked, tollbooth, police officer, red light, 8 in the morning, 5 in the evening, lunch time. A mass of cars, the helplessness of being stuck, not able to get one's vehicle through the endless mass of metal to arrive quickly at the desired destination. Patience turning to frustration, the realization of the impossibility of movement, horn beeps, attempts to get over, let a driver in, to gain a few more feet, anything that allows movement, the essence of transportation. Transportation, movement, an element common in every language, possibly believably the most, getting from here to there. From here to there, an analysis of movement, one that predates fiction, one that explores base material, one that is simple.

"We had entered an immense traffic jam. From the junction of the motorway and western avenue to the ascent ramp of the flyover the traffic lanes were packed with vehicles, windshields leaching out the molten colors of the sun setting above the western suburbs of London. Brake lights, flared in the evening air, glowing in the huge pool of cellulosed bodies. Vaughn sat with one arm out of the passenger window. He slapped the door impatiently, pounding the panel with his fist. To our right the high wall of a double-decker airline coach formed a cliff of faces. The passengers at the windows resembled rows of the dead looking down at us from the galleries of a columbarium. The enormous energy of the 20th century, enough to drive the planet into a new orbit around a happier star, was being expended to maintain this immense motionless pause" (*Crash*, 151).

Vaughn an existence not in *Crash*, but a cultural identity that flows through Ballard's fiction, the new dromoscopic citizen in a landscape removed from a central spatial landscape, home on the road, home only in time. Dirty, perverse, angry, violent: a product of availability and the honesty of information. Vaughn's backseat filled with hundreds of car crash photos, medical reports, crash histories, his mind filled with stories (his car the same make of Kennedy's in Dallas). Vaughn's "I," once a televised personality, has been lost in the mirrored detached reflection of the televised body, has become a personality crafted around an available reflection that reaches beyond possible awareness by technology fragmenting his image through televised pauses, second by second overviews to a manipulatable body double other. Identity in the external replicated image of the body:

"The apartment was dominated by Vaughan's evident narcissism-the walls of the studio, bathroom and kitchen were covered with photographs of himself, stills form his television programmes, half-plate-prints from newspaper photographers, polaroid snapshots of himself on location...Vaughn was self consciously absorbed in these fading images, straightening their curling corners as if frightened that when they finally vanished his own identity would also cease to matter" (*Crash*, 168).

"An introverted tourism, the movements of his body appear and disappear in their dromoscopic rhythm...The actor turns back upon himself in order to hunt down his errors and his imperfections; hoping to attain himself as the target, he never takes his aim off himself, memorizing, he hopes, certain reflexes, the result of an 'image of the body' doubled...A new type off ostracism, the actor possesses himself henceforth in the measure of to which he accepts being dispossessed of his immediate consciousness for the sake of the sole sense of vision, but a vision which is remote and distant" (*Negative Horizon*, 124).

Vaughn: a body outside of the body, a being without a body. Vaughn, an idol whose behavior is the behavior of the age: watching. The situation, presence in the vehicle, "I" unable to drive because of the jam, unable to work because of the limitation of the metal and glass of the vehicle, though still having to act through necessary expenditure because of being a product of expenditure. Stuck in the car, Vaughn hits the car, impatiently, often, spending the energy in his tank, his cells pistons pumping, like the man in the asylum cell, slowly running up the walls, slowly turning into the dead face of the tourist, the extreme traveler that lives an existence of non-stop direction, an existence where all responsibility is removed from the itinerary.

The Airport Landscape

"On the first afternoon I had barely recognized the endless landscape of concrete and structural steel that extended from the motorways to the south of the airport, across its vast runways to the new apartment systems along Western Avenue. Our own apartment house at Drayton Park stood a mile to the north of the airport in a pleasure island of modern housing units, landscaped filling stations and supermarkets, shielded from the distant bulk of London by an access spur of the northern circular motorway which flowed past us on its elegant concrete pillars"(*Crash*, 48).

Ballard returned from the hospital after his crash with Helen Remington is awakened by the pain and violence of his happening. Re-born with new perception, Ballard's common association with his world is gone. An association dominated by the pattern of home to supermarket, supermarket to filling station, filling station to home. A patterned dominated by driving pattern established by the constraints of the road, the highest speeds able to be reached, the least amount of stoplights present. Constraints of the road, the highest speeds able to be reached, dominated by Convenience and Desire. Convenience and Desire shaping urban planning specifically to remove the traffic jam, to keep materials flowing, creating a logistical system so intricately planned for that one doesn't have to live at all, i.e. take care.

Ballard keeps the novel centered around the airport, the extreme model of contemporary life, a landscape designed specifically for the receiving and expulsion of the maximum amount of matter without creating a traffic jam, an architecture shaped by maximum utility:

"In fact, between the automobile, the escalator, and the plane cabin, we pass from one technological vehicle to another without any significant transition. We see the same change across the Atlantic with...Dallas airport which resembles a computer. It covers a surface comparable to that of the Parisian centre and will allow for the turnover of an equivalent population, 10 to 15 million passengers per year" (*Negative Horizon*, 98).

Understanding the importance of this location is critical to only to understanding *Crash*, but to contemporary society. The airport is a harbor, a place to land and depart from. To take a break from transiting. The central location of the airport in *Crash* exhibits a world that is becoming impermanent, where the lucid, the flux, the moving through, has become more common than the dwelling, a dwelling that is necessary for "we." A life that comes into existence only when it stops to land. A life in the sky that is there for a moment, a weekend, and then is off again to a new location, a new vacation, a new business trip, having no regularity, no single point of reflection: "When we know that every day there are over one hundred thousand people in the air, we can consider it a foreshadowing of a future society..." (*Pure War*, 65).

This single point of reflection has always been the city, and the city and the harbor were once united, the harbor at the city, the city at the harbor. In *Crash* the airport harbor is separate from the city, and so challenges the city, takes away from the city's unique status, this status being the market place, the common language. Nowhere in *Crash* is a description of the London skyline, the city streets, dark alleyways where prostitutes stand: locations that out of daily necessity demand having a central location, a place that must be visited in taking care. Instead of the London skyline there is the description of long-term multi story parking lots, suburbs, instead of cobblestone streets, on ramps and exit ramps, instead of dark alleyways where one would engage in illicit behavior, this honorable location in *Crash* is airport maintenance roads. Ballard's writing presents a new landscape in *Crash*, one that characterizes the shift from the political center that was once the city. A shift that occurs from Convenience and Desire creating availability: ***shielded** from the distant bulk of London by an **access** spur of the northern circular motorway.*

Logistics and the Accident

An access road is an opening, a space that allows for material to fall into it, to fill it, to move through. An access is an opening, which is when the limit has been surpassed and possibility materializes. The access road bypasses restraint, which is always the jam, immobility, the limit. Following the merge onto the access road, the driver experiences a series of events, a series of events that are manifested by directed expenditure unfolding in a systematic behavior. The access road is a created opening, one that is introduced later into infrastructure, one that is planned for. This behavior, planning for, the placement of the road to maximize flow, is logistics.

Logistics means the organized purposeful direction of matter. Logistical planning became prevalent in times of war when the size of war became so large that the management of war came to include not just troop placement, but arming, transporting, and feeding these numbers. When war comes to involve millions of individuals, logistics is the solution to directing these large populations. How war and logistics relates to *Crash* and access roads is that logistics does not discriminate with matter. A million directed individuals traveling in their cars between home and work in times of peace is to logistics that same as one million armed individuals traveling between battlefields in times of war. Logistics gives modern wars their flavor, and gives the night sky its hundreds of shooting stars that constantly take off and land, the millions of lights that start and stop traffic, the single computer that runs the trains on clock time in a national railway system. Logistical planning is deceptively present underneath, at the moment of expenditure, influencing, enraging, pleasuring, and introducing the horrible violence of the past century into life.

The violence of logistics is the violence of speed. Logistics creates routes that involve the fastest times. The route, the access road, seeks to resemble the straight line, the shortest distance between point A and B. The shortest distance destroys the possibility of choice, a choice that can't be chosen because of the speed of travel, the single addictive road that by passing all the surrounding restraints grants a sense of *freedom* in the illusion of movement. Underneath speed there is force: force = mass x acceleration. The vehicle traveling through the landscape, warping the grasp of "World," is no different from a projectile, is a projectile that upon impact explodes reality into physical possibilities that were never possible before. The secret that resides within speed is possibility. As speeds increase so do the possibilities of what may occur. From a body that can only be hurt by the impact of falling to the ground during walking speed to a body that is exploding, torn in two at the waist, entrails tossed about the pavement, from the violence that is contained when the force of the vehicle hits them in the crash. The monstrosities that are possible, always forgotten until they are materialized by a certain speed:

"Almost every conceivable violent confrontation between the automobile and its occupants was listed: mechanisms of passenger ejection, the geometry of kneecap and hip-joint injuries, deformation of passenger compartments in head-on and rear-end collisions, injuries sustained in accidents at roundabouts, at trunkroad intersections, at the junctions between access roads and motorway intersections, the telescoping mechanisms of car-bodies in front-end collisions, abrasive injuries formed in roll-overs, the amputation of limbs by roof assemblies and door sills during roll-over, facial injuries caused by dashboard and window trim, scalp and cranial injuries caused by rear-view mirrors and sun-visors, whiplash injuries in rear-end collisions, first and second degree burns in accidents involving the rupture and detonation of fuel tanks, chest injuries caused by steering column impalements, abdominal injuries caused by faulty seat-belt adjustment, second-order collisions between front-seat and rear-seat passengers, cranial and spinal injuries caused by ejection through windshields, the graded injuries to the skull caused by variable windshield glasses, injuries to minors, both children and infants in arms, injuries caused by prosthetic limbs, injuries caused within cars fitted with invalid controls, the complex self-amplifying injuries of single and double amputees, injuries caused by specialist automobile accessories such as radio players, cocktail cabinets and radio telephones, the injuries caused by manufacturers' medallions, safety belt pinions and quarter-window latches" (*Crash*, 132-133).

Preventing the Accident

"Every technology produces, provokes, programs a specific accident....The invention of the boat was the invention of the shipwrecks. The invention of the steam engine and the locomotive was the invention of derailments. The invention of the highway was the invention of the three hundred cars colliding in five minutes. The invention of the airplane was the invention of the plane crash" (*Pure War*, 32).

"The electric winches which propelled the catapult began to drum at the rails, the cables tautening...with a loud jerk, the motor cycle sped down the track, its cables clanking between the metal rails...a harsh whipping noise came toward us, the sound of the motoring coils skating along the grass beside the rail. There was a violent metallic explosion as the motorcycle struck the front of the saloon car. The two vehicles veered sideways towards the line of startled spectators...the motor cycle and its driver sailed over the bonnet of the car and struck the windshield, then careened across the roof in a black mass of fragments. The car plunged ten feet back on its housers. It came to rest astride the rails. The bonnet, windshield and roof had been crushed by the impact" (*Crash*, 124-125).

In the simulated accident no one is hurt. The driver is a
dummy. The cars are on a closed course, in a science lab. The
simulated crash attempts to fragment the accident down to a
point of no possibility. Creating in the point of no possibility a
reality where there is no possibility of the accident occurring,
where the accident would be, safety standards are instead.
Crashing over and over and over again, the vehicle is finally
deemed safe to travel at high speeds. The World, as the car,
takes on the structure of the car's safety standards, limiting
possibility to match the safety standards characteristics of the
vehicle. By removing accidents the vehicle is initiated into the
relativity of speeds, of being able to merge into the particular
flux of vehicles, becoming one with speed limits. Safety seeks
to freeze reality from falling out of hand, into the chaos of the
accident. Vehicles becoming more and more stable against
accidents, creating an environment where the accidents never
occur. The transistors forgetting about the violence all the
while present in the world's motion, in their daily life, though,
waiting to emerge when unsuspecting for a second the
transistor becomes forgetful, becomes lost, looks down from
the wheel, crosses the road, violence emerging suddenly
through a crack, a monster force emerging, a force that
increases with all the increases of transit capabilities, bending
metal and deforming the body.

Movement, Stability, and Myth

Movement is present until movement can no longer occur.
When limitation is reached there is *Stability*. Upon limitation
reached, movement reflects backwards, gaining the
appearance of movement, directing stability to move. The
characteristic of displacement: moving over, through, against,
alongside. *Movement* first to *Stability*, then movement through
Stability:

"First, living matter receives this energy and accumulates it
within the limits given by the space that is available to it. It
then radiates or squanders it, but before devoting an

appreciable share to this radiation it makes maximum use of it
for growth. Only the impossibility of continuing growth makes
way for squander. Hence the real excess does not begin until
the growth of the individual or group has reached its limits"
(*The Accursed Share*, 29).

After founding the origin of the awareness of a stable world
Movement takes on a secondary characteristic, that of the
movement that moves through the World of *Stability*. The first
component establishes the stable characteristic of the world
that is moved through. The second component establishes the
movement that occurs through the world. *Movement*, the
accumulating of the energy prior to excess, is always primary
to *Stability*, the excess of energy that buys the possible, and in
the crash accumulation is remembered in the exhaustion of
possibility, the finding of seething immanence. The crash
upon impact returns *Movement* to its primary place before
Stability, awakening the victim that has been ignorant to the
violence underneath stability to the other outside of stable
Reason.

Crash is the Story of individuals taking empowered action in
response to violence. Of entering into the violence, channeling
spirit. This channeling of spirit can be seen in *The Recreation
of a Spectacular Road Side Accident* that occurs in *Crash*.
This scene is short in Ballard's fiction, but deeply enthralling
in Cronenberg's film rendition. Wonderfully narrated by
Vaughn in the film, he describes the story leading up to James
Dean's auto accident, and how in the recreation about to be
performed, authenticity to the accident is kept.

*VAUGHAN: The first star of our show is Little Bastard-,
James Dean's racing Porsche. He named it after himself, and
had his racing number, 130, painted on it...*

*The second star is stuntman and former race driver - Colin
Seagrave, who will drive our replica of James Dean's car...*

*I myself shall play the role of James Dean's racing mechanic,
Rolf Wotherich, sent over from the Porsche factory in*

Zuffenhausen, Germany. This mechanic was himself fated to die in a car crash in Germany twenty-six years later. And the third and in some ways most important party, the college student Donald Turnupseed, played by movie stuntman Brett Trask....

Turnupseed was on his way back to his home in Fresno for the weekend. James Dean was on his way to an automobile race in Salines, a dusty town in northern California. The two would only meet for one moment, but it was a moment that would create a Hollywood legend...

You'll notice that we are not wearing helmets or safety padding of any kind, and our cars are not equipped with roll cages or seat belts. We depend solely on the skill of our drivers for our safety so that we can bring you the ultimate in authenticity. All right, here we go. The fatal crash of James Dean! (*Crash*, Cronenberg).

The recreation is not a recreation of physical events, but of myth. Myth is Reason in *Stability*, as are the characters (the heroes), involved in the Myth. James Dean the Hero exists. James Dean the person has no existence. James Dean the celebrity has a power and significance beyond Colin Seagrave, Rolf Wotherich, and Brett Trask, who are the actors, the imitators, like James Dean the person. And even these individuals, Colin Seagrave, Vaughn, and Brett Trask, who are on film, have their identity overshadowed by their Mythical screen presence, their daily existence insignificant below their role. The Hero's existence is created as a defense to violence, within the *Stability* secondary to *Movement*. Ballard's identity is small, changing, petty, and insignificant, but Dean's like a star, persists in the sky unchallenged. I change, suffer, but Dean doesn't. Though Dean's vessel dies, so his loss becomes sacred, a legend, and the ability of Dean's identity to live on through history is allowed. The recreation of Dean's accident though, like all of *Crash*, is perversion, because the recreation seeks to recreate the destruction of the stable identity. As a work it is not interested in safety, it is interested in accidents and accidents are that which is naught sought.

The introduction of the recreation first told by Vaughn casts the spell allowing the events to be understood as the James Dean myth as they unfold in front of the audience. The story founded around Dean, the objects present leech off of Dean's identity, and share in his sacred power. The participants sans helmet, safety padding, roll cage or seat belt, cannot be seen as mere imitators, *mimes*. Their actions seek to authentically recreate the crash, tear apart the stability, and show the violence that is beneath the stability and do so because they do crash without any limitations or precautions. The crash occurs, and in the clash of steel everything the audience sees changes. James Dean has a collision, not Seagrave, Little Bastard is ruined, not the modeled crash car. The eroticism of the moment, resting between *Movement* and *Stability,* turns identity away from the identity of the conquering Hero and showcases the force of the accident.

The extent of the violence cannot be understood from observation, only experienced as a victim. Violence is personable. In violence "I" confront a force greater than me, that of *Movement*, the immanence which is primary to *Stability*. To cope with the violence the immanence of the event is turned into something else, Reason. Becoming one with the violence, rather than letting it act on being, being acts out of violence, as Reason. The violence underneath the crash, that the crash shows, cannot be prevented since violence, as a force of movement, is always prior to stability, ready to re-emerge. Violence is subverted by being turned into a cult. Helpless, the passenger becomes a follower of the crash, the crash becomes worshiped as a totem. Violence accepted, and in acceptance, becomes force that is directed, manipulated, harnessed, and allows being to act upon the world through Reason, in *Stability*.

Violence is released within movement. The body moves, it is violent. The body does not move, it must move, expenditure, violence occurs to the body in the suppression of the movement, psychological restraint: red light, green light. The transportation system is an incredibly violent system. Organizing, displacing, signaling, the body's existence shares the same structure, constraint. The roads that provide freedom of vehicle movement prevent bodily movement. To survive the movement on the roads, the body turns in on itself, suppressing, naturally cultivating excess energy into a reserve that can't be spent. Motionless the body sits, removed from pain by an increasingly adapting maximum comfort system, allowing the body to forget the pain of the violence, the body. In the car, the bus, the plane, the extreme turn inward to a zombie tourist. Supply lines reach across the globe, the connection of transit systems showing the existence of Pure War, matter organized and directed, transiting that never ends. A world micromanaged, that to function must remove man from man, treat man as object. This tyranny of the transport system seen already in its dealing with the transportation of large populations, the only way to prevent a jam is to turn man into freight and ship him off to depots, Auschwitz.

Crash is the derailing of this system, the destruction of time and Reason, freeing being from red light, green light, of the comfort that surrounds the body causing the body to forget the body. The awakening from the structured life style, those dead faces, the skyline of cement and steel. Crashing, the erotic of the moment is found, the immanence is fallen into, which expels the individual out of homogeneity, out of the cult, which grants the individual the ability to grasp his/her otherness, and to start a fresh in anguish, and seek, using violence, a world that they are no longer part of, that they are heterogeneous to.

Works Cited

F. Bacon, *The New Organon* (Cambridge: Cambridge University Press, 2000)

J. Ballard, *Crash* (New York: The Noonday Press, 1973)

J. Ballard and D. Cronenberg, *Crash* (New Line Home Video 1998)

G. Bataille, *The Accursed Share: Vol. 1* trans. Robert Hurley (New York: Zone Books, 1991)

G. Bataille, *Death and Sensuality* (New York: Ballantine Books, 1962)

G. Bataille, *Theory of Religion* trans. Robert Hurley (New York: Zone Books, 1992)

R. Caillois, *Man and the Sacred* (Chicago: University of Illinois Press, 2001)

G. Delluze and F. Guattari, *Anti-Oedipus: Capitalism and Schizophrenia* trans. Brian Massumi (Minneapolis: University of Minnesota Press, 1983)

M. Heidegger, *Being and Time* trans. Joan Stambaugh (New York: State University of New York Press, 1996)

M. Heidegger, *An Introduction to Metaphysics* (Fredericksburg: Yale University Press, Inc. 1959)

M, Heidegger, *Poetry, Language, Thought* (New York: Harper & Row, 1971)

M. Heidegger, *Questions Concerning Technology and Other Essays* (New York, Harper and Row, 1977)

M. Mauss, *General Theory of Magic* (London: Routledge Classics, 2001)

J. Nancy, *Being Singular Plural* trans. Robert Richardson, Anne O'Bryne (Stanford: Stanford University Press, 2000)

P. Virilio, *Negative Horizon* trans. Michael Degener (New York: Continuum, 2005)

P. Virilio, S. Lotringer *Pure War* trans. Mark Polizotti (New York: Semiotext(e), 1983)

Apocalypse Forever Part 7: Paul Virilio and the Tale of Sound and Fury, Signifying Nothing

Jon Thrower

It was Grandfather's and when Father gave it to me he said I give you the mausoleum of all hope and desire; it's rather excruciatingly apt that you will use it to gain the reducto absurdum of all human experience which you can fit your individual needs no better that it fitted his or his father's. I give it to you not that you may remember time, but that you might forget it now and then for a moment and not spend all your breath trying to conquer it. Because no battle is ever won he said. They are not even fought. The field only reveals to man his own folly and despair, and victory is an illusion of philosophers and fools.

William Faulkner – *The Sound and the Fury.* 1929.

William Faulkner's *The Sound and the Fury* is one of those works of high modernist fiction, like Joyce's *Ulysses*, or Pound's *Cantos*, which many claim reveal the root-structure of postmodernism to come through stream-of-consciousness narrative and fractal use of time and character as memory takes the form of straight narrative and vice versa. Overall the work is a tragedy in the sense of both Greek drama and Shakespeare.

Paul Virilio, cultural theorist, urbanist, student of the university of war, explicator of disaster and the accident has produced many thought-provoking texts and ideas through his long life. One of the fields with which he is most concerned is dromology (the science of speed), which is intimately linked with conceptions of space and time.

This examination will use these theoretical perspectives of Paul Virilio to reveal the depth of this tragedy of the literary character of Quentin Compson and the ways in which time and space contribute to the downfall of this young man who represents the hope of survival for the Compson family, and the South, in the second section of the novel.

The Quentin Section (as it is commonly known) or June Second, 1910 (more appropriately) begins with, "When the shadow of the sash appeared on the curtains it was between seven and eight o'clock and then I was in time again, hearing the watch." Here we have Quentin in his bed in the dorm waiting inactively for the day to come. He is noticing the effect of the sun rising and the resulting movement of the shadow. But he does not want the sun to come. As Epicurus said (and Virilio quotes on the website "The War and Peace Project), "Time is the accident to end all accidents." The measurement of time here is of course symbolized by the sun's movements through the morning, but it signifies not just the passage of time, but the passing by of a life. The sun is as a bell calling Quentin to his doom.

We should note here the setting: Harvard University, Cambridge, MA. Harvard is the oldest institution of higher learning in the United States and the oldest corporation. It is significant in the aspect of Quentin because of his source, his beginning in the South. And we must note the importance of history here. It is the vanquished South after the end of the Civil War, and the fall of aristocratic, plantation society from which Quentin's entire family history has evolved. The family has sold much of the old plantation land to send the young student to Harvard where they hope he will be the golden son (sun) who will return them to their previous glories. But Quentin's fate has long ago been decided. It is because of the racism and avarice of the slave-owning South that he has been doomed. And the space between Jefferson and Harvard could never be great enough to overcome the deeds of the past. In fact, it's greatness (spatially) further illustrates this complication. Virilio writes in *Open Sky*, "Loss of sight or, rather, 'loss of ground' in a new kind of fall that is also a form of pollution of expanse, of the 'art of the journey' practiced by the nomad, a peculiar form of vertigo brought on by the depth of field of the apparent horizon of the spectacle of the world" (33). We can see that the Compson family has lost both sight and ground in their quest to take control of the future and attempt to return to an impossible past. Quentin is reluctant to take the role as the golden calf of his family. He is haunted by his sister and his sensitivities cause him incredible difficulties and eventually a madness from which his vertigo will spiral out of control.

In this particular scene, the reader is thrust into the problem of time. We are given over to the part of the book which takes place out of the sequence which is itself out of sequence. This section, part two, takes place on June 2, 1910; outside of the out-of-sequence of the others (part one: April 7, 1928; part three: April 6, 1928; and part four: April 8, 1928). So this particular scene finds itself thrust from the spectrum of the rest of the narratives. Yet in the particular scene we are looking at, the primary context is memory, which serves as another thrust away from (and into) the real-time nature of the event.

Again, in *Open Sky*, Virilio writes, "[There is] a true crisis in the temporal dimension of immediate action. Following the crisis in 'whole' spatial dimensions and the resultant rise of 'fractal' dimensions, we will soon see a crisis, in short, in the temporal dimension of the present moment" (14). And while this quote takes place between the intonation of the concept of "tele-optical intervals," and "time-light" (the time of the speed of light), concepts which are fairly new to us now, not to mention in 1910/1929, the concepts themselves need not necessarily be limited to the technological moment of the now and can shed light on a fictional account which, in my view, can tell us a lot about the conditions of life, in any period. Going back to the quotation, Virilio traces the movement from the whole to the fractal to the present, specifically the "crisis moment" of the present.

A wide view of the June 2, 1910 section of the Faulkner novel reveals a young Quentin Compson, on the morning of his suicide. This last day and in fact the entire history and heritage of Quentin Compson is a crisis moment. He is a child of the reconstruction of the South after the Civil War. His formerly aristocratic family is in shambles, just like the geopolitical region. A large portion of the family "plantation" has been sold off to send Quentin to Harvard, though he is reluctant to go. Quentin (and indeed his entire family) is a symbol of the decline of the South. Much like a syllogism beginning with a faulty premise, each generation of the family further illustrates this doomed blueprint set by the family's namesake, General Compson, a Confederate Civil War 'hero.' As critic May Brown notes, "[Quentin's] failure to fulfill these obligations reveals not only his own limitations but also the failure of his heritage to provide values by which he can live."

More specifically, on this particular day in Cambridge, Quentin is engrossed in his life's problems, though in a very abstract manner. He lies in bed while listening (and not) to the watch his father gave him noticing the moment "when the shadow of the sash appeared on the curtains," a.k.a. the beginning of the day. In fact, the nightmare of time plays a central role in the entire episode, whether it be from this moment at the beginning of his last day, to the memory of his sister (and his concern for her virginity) and his belief that he has committed an incest, to his brother Benjy, preserved in a mental disease which holds him in an embrace of time from which he cannot escape, to the gift of the watch from his father and the infernal, negative speech about time.

Intertextually speaking, we can look back to the source of the book's title in Macbeth's speech in Act 5 for further illuminations on this problem with time.

"Life's but a walking shadow, a poor player, That struts and frets his hour upon the stage, And then is heard no more. It is a tale Told by an idiot, full of sound and fury, Signifying nothing (1069).

The quotation further secures the focus on this subject with which Virilio is so fascinated. One thing that stands out at this particular moment is the notion of the measurement of time. While we can measure time by seconds, minutes, hours, etc. we cannot measure time by lives. What is measured in the temporal division of lives is history; another concept for which Virilio's ideas hold a certain significance. Yet what Macbeth here notes is that life is a tale signifying nothing. He is, of course, speaking from his own fatalistic position following the witches' prediction and his betrayal of Duncan and the series of events following. Yet, much like the faulty syllogism example above, we can see the life of the Compson family and the particular example at hand, the doomed Quentin. And so, these three literary minds come to a point of fusion. When Quentin's father says, "I give you the mausoleum of all hope and desire." And Shakespeare says "[Life] is a tale...full of sound and fury, signifying nothing." And Virilio quotes Epicurus' "time is the accident to end all accidents." So time may be a mausoleum, and the be-all end-all accident, but it is really a faulty concept of measurement that we have designed as a means of attempting to solidify ground in a reality which is itself tenuous. And this, obviously, is itself faulty and will result in tragedy as time and life with it plummets ever forward, just as Quentin's body does (with pockets weighted with flatirons) into the Charles River.

And while Virilio, in *The Accident of Art*, bemoans the notion that art has forgotten tragedy, or that "... it does not recognize death and suffering. Consequently it ends up being dead itself" (24). However, in Faulkner's novel, this is not the case. As critic Warwick Wadlington notes, "*The Sound and the Fury* shows that the standard of tragedy contains the logic of its own failure."

As the section progresses toward that inevitable moment in the Charles, Quentin has destroyed the family watch, avoided seeing the correct time in the watchmaker, been arrested for a crime he did not commit, written his suicide notes, and purchased flatirons to ballast his body. But he is understandably driving himself mad in this tragic movement through time, despite his vein attempts to stop it. As Virilio noted in an interview with Louise Wilson of CTheory, "This is the accident of the body, a de-corporation. The body is torn and disintegrated... The mad person is wounded by his or her distorted relationship to the real." Note here the stream-of-consciousness writing, lacking both punctuation and capitalization, in the end of the section, where Quentin's madness has reached its peak. The final rant is only two sentences composed of 858 words as his memory of his father's words float into and out of his own attempt to convince himself that his suicide is inevitable. And it concludes with another reference to the "mausoleum of all hope and desire."

"you will remember that for you to go to harvard has been your mothers dream since you were born and no compson has ever disappointed a lady and i temporary it will be better for me for all of us and he every man is the arbiter of his own virtues but let no man prescribe for another man's wellbeing and i temporary and he was the saddest word of all there is nothing else in the world it's not despair until time it's not even time until it was."

The repetition of the phrase, "i temporary," which echoes his mentally handicapped brother Benjy's time-trapped speech, and returns to the point above in which life trapped in the measurement of days is cursed to go through with the preset accident toward disaster. This lowercase "i temporary" illustrates the fact that he will capitalize on his temporary nature by bringing about his own destruction and thus dwell in the mausoleum of his father's speech, the mausoleum of time, no longer. Because, "it's not despair until time, it's not even time until it was," reinforces this folly in the effort to set up a template with which to record and measure time, connecting and reaching back to the idea of the faulty premise of his familial heritage. In this quirky irony it is true that one has not actually lived a life until one is no longer living. And thus, Quentin is an end point, but his unraveling toward this point follows a special Virilian logic. The contraption of Quentin is uncoiling, becoming something he always/already was. His destiny: fulfilling the Virilian logic of disaster.

Works Cited

Brown, May Cameron. "The Language of Chaos: Quentin Compson in the Sound and the Fury." *American Literature*. 51.4 (1980). pp 544-553.

S. Lotringer, & P. Virilio. *The Accident of Art*. trans. Michael Taormina. New York: Semiotext(e), 2005.

The Complete Works of William Shakespeare. New York: Gramercy, 1975.

The Sound and the Fury: a Hypertext Edition. Ed. Stoicheff, Muri, Deshaye, et al. Updated Mar. 2003. U of Saskatchewan. Accessed 18 Dec.2008. http://www.usask.ca/english/faulkner.

P. Virilio, *Open Sky* trans. Julie Rose (London: Verso, 1997)

P. Virilio, "Red Alert in Cyberspace." The Information Technology, War and Peace Project. Accessed 3 Jan. 2009. http://www.watsoninstitute.org/infopeace/vy2k/red-alert.cfm

Wadlington, Warwick. "The Sound and the Fury: A Logic of Tragedy." *American Literature*. 53.3 (1981) pp 409-423

Wilson, Louise. "Cyberwar, God and Television: Interview with Paul Virilio." CTheory. Eds. Arthur and Marilouise Kroker. 1, Dec. 1994. http://www.ctheory.net/articles.aspx?id=62.

PART III: La Version Originelle

Séance-I
L'introduction à l'écologie grise

« Qu'attendons-nous lorsque nous n'aurons plus besoin d'attendre pour arriver? Nous attendons la venue de ce qui demeure. » Paul Virilio

Je suis urbaniste et philosophe. Non par modestie, mais parce que la philosophie est née dans la ville. Je ne suis non seulement urbaniste et essayiste, c'est ma meilleure définition, et pas du tout philosophe, mais aussi claustrophobe. Vous allez comprendre pourquoi.

Au moment où l'on parle tellement d'écologie verte, c'est-à-dire celle de l'épuisement de la géodiversité, celle du réchauffement climatique, etc. Mais cette présentation que je vais faire devant vous, est approximative. La dromologie et sa dromopshère, c'est-à-dire, l'accélération de la réalité et pas simplement, l'accélération de l'histoire, cette dromologie n'est qu'une approximation. Et selon moi, elle ne sera jamais une réponse absolue, pourquoi? Parce qu'elle touche à la relativité même. Je rappelle, la vitesse n'est pas un phénomène, c'est la relation entre les phénomènes. C'est la relativité même. A partir du moment où on se trouve dans le langage mathématique, on ne peut pas entrer dans la précision de la dromologie.

A Valence, un professeur qui présentait sa thèse essayait d'illustrer la dimension approximative de mon travail. Ce n'est pas par modestie. L'approximation est pour moi, dans le domaine de la vitesse, un phénomène capital. Il n'y a pas une précision de la vitesse. (Il y a un phénomène entre le temps et l'espace) Donc, la dromologie n'est pas une théorie close, complète. C'est évident, vitesse et accident sont liés, d'où cette approximation. C'est sûrement une discipline ouverte et offerte à d'autres interprétations. D'où le rapport avec l'écologie verte, celle qui est liée à la nature. L'écologie grise,

quant à elle, est ouverte au cosmos et à la culture, ici, aucune
maîtrise n'est possible.

S'il y avait un professeur, un philosophe qui rédigeait un traité
de la dromologie je pense que je ne le lirais pas, non pas par
orgueil, parce que ça ne m'intéresserait pas. Pourquoi? Parce
que la relativité nous amène à étudier deux ordres de grandeur,
la grandeur des distances, de la science, et les disciplines
mathématiques..., il y aussi la pauvreté, la grandeur de la
faiblesse, les deux ordres sont liés. D'où un intérêt pour la
finitude et pour ceux qui exhument, le travail sur l'écologie
grise est souvent analysé par ceux qui me suivent comme un
travail apocalyptique, ce qui n'est pas vrai. La dromologie,
n'est pas la fin du monde, je dis souvent que le concept "la fin
du monde" est un concept sans avenir.

Non, ce qui m'intéresse, c'est "la finitude du monde". Qu'est-
ce que la finitude simplement? C'est qu'une pomme n'est
qu'une pomme. C'est qu'un homme, n'est qu'un homme et
que le monde n'est qu'un monde. C'est ça la finitude. Donc,
mon intérêt aujourd'hui à travers la dromosphère, le passage et
l'accélération de l'histoire et l'accélération de la réalité à
travers les nouvelles technologies, c'est la forclusion du
monde, l'enclosure du monde. La pollution des distances de
temps est beaucoup plus grave, selon moi, que la pollution des
substances matérielles. La pollution de la grandeur nature du
monde à coté de celle de la nature, écologie verte. C'est la
pollution de la nature. L'écologie grise c'est la pollution de la
grandeur nature et je vous rappelle que je suis architecte plus
que philosophe et que l'histoire de grandeur des proportions,
des dimensions est un élément essentiel. L'étendue, la taille ou
les dimensions propres sont des éléments qui ne sont pas pris
en compte réellement dans les phénomènes. Je vous rappelle
que, petite digression, j'ai publié trois livres. En 1976,
L'insécurité du territoire qui déjà préfaçait le crépuscule des
lieux. En 1984 en rendant hommage à Orwell, j'ai publié
L'espace critique. Et, en 1990, *L'inertie polaire*. Le premier
qui parle du crépuscule des lieux. D'où cette introduction de la
contraction temporelle de la géosphère habitable en commun.

C'est ce qu'on appelle dans l'informatique la contraction
temporelle.

Je répète que, la contraction temporelle, réduit à rien ou
presque, l'étendue même du globe de la géosphère habitable,
du monde commun. Il n'y a qu'un seul monde : la
dromosphère réduit à rien la géosphère, la biosphère. Le temps
réel, l'instantané de télécommunication, et la mise en œuvre
de l'internet, etc., est un temps de la géodiversité, et de la
biodiversité. Quand on parle de la pollution, on parle souvent
de la pollution matérielle. C'est tellement faux. C'est
l'urbaniste et l'architecte qui le dit : il y la pollution des
distances de la grandeur nature, il n'y a pas de grandeur sans
dimension. Il n'a pas d'objets sans proportions. Il n'y a pas
d'homme sans dimensions. C'est finalement le matérialisme,
sans oublier la notion des échelles de grandeur. La notion
d'échelles. Et de proportions des choses dans l'espace et le
temps de différentes substances. C'est très étonnant comment
on lie facilement la nature à la culture mais on oublie
facilement la grandeur. C'est toute la question que j'évoque
dans mon livre qui s'appelle *L'espace critique* qui donne son
nom à ma collection dans laquelle étaient publiés Baudrillard,
et Guattari, etc. L'espace critique n'est pas seulement un
temps, l'instant, c'est aussi l'espace. L'architecte, que je suis,
met en œuvre toute sa construction matérielle, en construisant
tout d'abord les proportions qui donnent la mesure de son
bâtiment. Il construit les proportions avant de construire des
pierres ou du béton. Le temps réel. Le continuum espace-
temps du monde subit une contraction temporelle, qui réduit à
rien ou presque l'étendue même du monde. Cela ne fait pas
mal, comme l'échauffement climatique ou l'épuisement de
l'eau.

Hélas, c'est autrement grave. Le temps réel est un séisme du
temps. Grand ou faible, cette étendue constitue la puissance de
l'être. Et maintenant j'ai un exemple très clair. Être un homme
c'est de mesurer en gros entre un et deux mètres, au maximum
entre un nain et un géant. Si un homme mesure 20 mètres de
haut, ce n'est pas un homme. C'est impensable. Tout est

comme ça. C'est étonnant jusqu'à quel point les proportions
ont disparues du monde moderne. D'où les deux ordres de
grandeur dont j'ai parlé tout à l'heure qui sont
équivalents. L'un est la partie faible de l'autre. Il y deux
ordres de grandeur : la grandeur de puissance, on parle en
particulier de la puissance de l'Amérique, c'est une réalité,
mais la grandeur de pauvreté est aussi une réalité de même
grandeur. Et ici les termes de mesure, et de démesure,
s'adressent à la restitution. Dans l'écologie grise, les termes de
mesure et de démesure s'adressent à la restitution, à la
rétention de l'étendue du monde. Dans l'écologie grise, les
termes de mesure et de démesure ne s'adressent pas à l'hyper-
en dehors de l'astrophysique, cosmique, mais la restriction à la
rétention soudaine de l'étendue du monde.

Le caractère démesuré de la contraction de l'écologie est celui
du transport. Le caractère démesuré de cette accélération de la
réalité du globe, de son continuum, conditionne non seulement
la nature c'est-à-dire les trajets et le déplacement, mais
autrement, la culture et l'histoire. L'histoire se contracte en
même temps que sa géographie. Là encore, je suis urbaniste et
je peux vous dire que l'histoire et la cité sont liées à une
contraction, celle de la cité, celle de la concentration, celle de
la globalisation, et c'est l'échec du succès des techno-sciences.
C'est un échec d'un succès et non pas un échec d'erreur. Cette
contraction, celle de l'accélération de la réalité, elle est l'échec
du succès des sciences opératoires du progrès. Je soutiens, et
en particulier dans un livre que j'écris qui s'appellera
Université du désastre, que la science subira un accident du
fait d'une finitude du monde, c'est-à-dire que la contraction
spatio-temporelle est conditionnée par les lieux de l'être et les
choses. La contraction temporelle n'est pas simplement les
transports et les délais *live* pour téléphoner, pour transmettre
par internet, c'est quoi? Ça concerne le savoir. La rétention de
l'espace-temps du monde concerne premièrement la science et
la philosophie. D'où cette idée de raconter l'accident des
substances chez Aristote. Il va y avoir, il y a déjà un accident
de connaissances. Les connaissances sont liées à l'étendue,
sont liées à la mesure du monde. Toute notre science est liée à

la géographie du monde. Pas simplement à l'histoire du savoir mais, à l'étendue même de ceux qui suivent tout le temps son savoir. D'où le besoin de l'université du désastre. Je veux parler de la peur, la claustrophobie dont j'ai parlé tout à l'heure. La peur de l'accélération n'est pas encore présente, mais certains claustrophobes ou asthmatiques ressentent déjà cette peur là. La peur d'épuiser la géodiversité du monde. Je vais vous donner un exemple. Je suis allé deux fois à Venise. Une ville extraordinaire. J'ai eu un ami qui me montrait tel et tel endroit. Il me dit qu'il faut aller voir encore d'autres sites et puis j'aurais tout vu, et j'ai dit non ! Je veux garder Venise inconnue pour pouvoir revenir. Quelque part je ne veux pas épuiser ce trésor. Je ne veux pas participer au crépuscule des lieux.

Par exemple, la connaissance des antipodes par le tourisme restreint fatalement cette étendue où éclate la puissance géophysique du monde. A part de ce saint monde, aucun autre monde n'est habitable pour l'instant. Et cette peur, cette angoisse, la claustrophobie qu'ont quelques adultes va bientôt devenir un phénomène de masses. Le crainte devant le grand enfermement écologique dont Foucault parle à propos des asiles, de l'univers carcéral, imaginez demain que ce sentiment de grand enfermement ne concerne plus seulement la mise en prison d'un individu ou un autre, mais la grande claustration d'un monde trop petit pour nous. C'est ça l'angoisse. Imaginez dans une ou deux générations: en fin de semaine, allez au cirque de Tokyo, manger un casse-croûte à New York, et le lendemain, recommencez, et tout ça pour un ou deux dollars. *Open Sky,* le voyage sera moins cher, imaginez ce monde où tout sera déjà là, déjà vu, déjà donné. Et, en France, le tourisme ne concerne pas que les personnes adultes, aujourd'hui, elle est localisée.

Cette inquiétude, elle est déjà présente, vous savez, dans les recherches de l'astrophysique concernant les exo-planètes, on voit la grande externalisation outre-monde du jour au lendemain. Je vous cite une phrase de Stephen Hawking, le grand astrophysicien anglais, « Dès lors que nous aurons des

perspectives sur d'autres planètes, notre avenir sera assuré. »
Autrement dit, notre avenir dépend des planètes habitables.
Dans le système solaire, dit-il, pour l'instant il faudra
cinquante mille ans pour arriver à un bon résultat. Avec les
technologies nouvelles, peut-être on peut rendre cet exploit
possible, mais le voyage durerait au moins six ans. Quand un
homme comme lui, un scientifique dit une phrase comme
celle-là, c'est-à-dire que l'avenir de l'humanité dépend d'une
colonisation outre-monde d'un monde qui n'existe pas sans
eau, sans air, la question relève de cette inquiétude, cette
claustrophobie. Elle est chez lui parce que c'est ce sur quoi il
travaille. Vous avez lu ces recherches sur les exo-planètes?

A l'aquarium de la Rochelle, on peut voir une exposition sur
les exo-océans. C'est quoi un exo-océan? C'est un océan
exotique. Alors, peut-être sur la lune Europe de la grande
planète Jupiter, il y aurait un océan sous la glace. C'est un
morceau de glace qui mesure des centaines de mètres et sous
la glace, il y aurait peut-être un océan. Comme le disait un
astrologue de la NASA, « L'océan a trop d'eau. Alors il y a
combien d'années lumières ? » Vous voyez l'étendue?

Je voudrais travailler, vous savez, sur les espaces de la
claustration. Lorsqu'on entend la phrase de Stephen Hawking
que j'ai citée tout à l'heure, « Dès lors que nous nous
désignerons d'autres planètes, notre avenir sera assuré. » Ça
veut dire que l'astrophysique est le substitut de la
géophysique. Pour moi c'est un délire. Le délire d'une science
privée de la conscience philosophique de l'échec du progrès.
L'échec du progrès, c'est l'échec de son succès face à la
finitude du monde. C'est l'échec de sa réussite spectaculaire.
Je ne suis pas contre le progrès, je dis que c'est
merveilleusement catastrophique. L'échec de la réussite
spectaculaire est dans tous les domaines: l'anthropologie,
l'énergie, les informations de la matière sauf dans celui de la
sagesse du discernement de la fin, le discernement de la
finitude. Cette réussite spectaculaire des sciences exactes, des
sciences opératoires, et non pas seulement du savoir, n'a pas
pris en compte la fin, la mort. La finitude donne l'effet que le

monde n'est qu'un monde, et que la science n'est qu'une
science limitée. Comme le dit quelqu'un, « la vérité
scientifique c'est une erreur en sursis. »

C'est pour ça que je ne peux pas ne pas travailler sur la vitesse
sans travailler sur l'accident. Vitesse et accident sont liés.
Nous allons terminer sur ce que j'appelle « l'accident intégral
». Les accidents scientifiques, technoscientifiques, ont été très
localisés. Par exemple auparavant, une bombe explosait
quelque part, la pollution d'un incendie était à *tel endroit*.
Aujourd'hui l'accident devient intégral. Il concerne l'étendue
du monde commun. On remplace l'étendue du monde par la
vitesse. C'est vraiment l'accident intégral. En remplaçant
l'étendue du monde par la vitesse c'est-à-dire celle du
transport ou bien celles des transmissions électromagnétiques,
sans provoquer un accident sériel, un accident intégral qui
concerne à la fois, des effets d'énergies cinétiques et ceux que
j'appelle des énergies cinématiques de l'accélération de la
réalité. Et donc, on bouleverse, fatalement l'histoire et sa
géographie. Le grand renfermement du 21ème siècle,
l'incarcération qui dépasse infiniment celui du 18ème siècle,
de l'ère panoptique dénoncée par Foucault, après avoir été
annoncée par Jeremy Bentham? C'est la grande question
aujourd'hui. C 'est quoi? Passer du *live*, c'est cette télé-
objectivité du monde. C'est *Google-Earth*. On est passé de la
mégalomanie à la mégalopsychie.

L'approche et l'étude de la dromosphère est celle de
l'accélération du réel. Le temps réel est encore sur l'espace
réel de la géographie. Ce que les anciens assiégés
dénommaient « la fièvre obsidionale » - la peur du grand
renfermement a un nom. Je rappelle que j'ai beaucoup
travaillé sur les stratégies liées à la guerre, aux sièges, etc. «
La fièvre obsidionale » je vous en donne un exemple
extraordinaire: le ghetto de Varsovie. Au sein du ghetto de
Varsovie, en plein hiver un journaliste remarquait que ça puait
le charbon et que toutes les fenêtres étaient ouvertes. Il
demandait aux gens pourquoi ils gardaient leurs fenêtres
ouvertes en plein hiver, et ils disaient, nous, on est déjà

assiégé et tu veux qu'on ferme les fenêtres? C'est ça « la fièvre obsidionale ». Sauf ici, la fièvre obsidionale est celle d'une ville: le ghetto.

Imaginez demain à l'échelle du monde l'état d'urgence d'une nouvelle technologie, qui est un état de siège du monde. État de déception, celle du progrès de la réalité, le progrès sur le transport, origine de la radio, origine des télécommunications, de la puce de radio fréquence. État de déception, État d'urgence, État de siège. Supprimer la liberté publique. Seulement il n'y pas de tyran qui les supprime. Ils sont supprimés par la claustration du monde. La forclusion du monde. Il n'y a plus besoin de tyran. Rassurez-vous, je ne suis pas désespéré. Je crois qu'il est temps d'ouvrir l'université du désastre. Il y a une phrase de Churchill qui dit qu'un optimiste voit une opportunité derrière chaque calamité.

Question: Ça me rappelle la mesure platonicienne.

Paul Virilio: Je suis un relativiste. Non, je pense simplement qu'on ne peut être architecte, urbaniste, c'est-à-dire un homme de la proportion en niant la mesure. Ce n'est pas une mesure morale de garder les choses, c'est la géophysique. Quand tu vois quelqu'un qui te plait, tu dis qu'elle possède de belles proportions, ce n'est pas une question de morale. Ceci dit, c'est vrai que la racine est là. Entre les Égyptiens et les Grecs on a la question de mesure. Non, je crois qu'on a oublié cette étendue. Cette idée qu'un homme, s'il mesure 1m60 ou 2 mètres, c'est un homme et si il mesure 20 mètres, ce n'est plus un homme. C'est tellement ridicule de dire ça, mais on dirait que ça n'est pas passé dans notre culture. Et c'est curieux ce déni du petit. Il y a de la grandeur comme des grains de blés incommensurables. La grandeur de l'atome, la grandeur des grains de blé, etc. Il y a une sorte de disqualification de ce qui est petit, de la grandeur de la petitesse et non pas la grandeur du petit. Il y a là quelque chose qui va dans le même sens que le déni de la pauvreté au profit de la richesse dans l'ordre de l'économie. Là, c'est l'économie de l'espace: les proportions et la géométrie, et l'autre c'est l'économie de biens. D'où la référence à la grandeur de la pauvreté. C'est Bossuet qui a parlé de l'importance de ces deux grandeurs: la grandeur de la pauvreté et la grandeur de la puissance sont inséparables. On est en train d'oublier la grandeur de la pauvreté, mais l'écologie va nous ramener à cet ordre qu'elle soit grise ou verte.

Question: D'après vous, on oublie la grandeur du petit et de la proportion, mais est-ce que c'est un oubli ou bien un raccourci auquel nous sommes devenus accros?

Paul Virilio: Ce n'est pas une question d'oubli, mais de colonisation. La colonisation est un phénomène qui dépasse la politique coloniale. Elle conquiert, elle exploite, elle dégage. C'est-à-dire que c'est la technologie qui favorise la colonie. La Marine, aujourd'hui, est l'astronautique, les vaisseaux qui vont sur d'autres planètes. On ne peut pas parler de la colonisation sans la grandeur de la puissance maritime et la grandeur de la puissance aérienne devenue astronautique etc. Donc, quelque part, l'idéologie coloniale fait partie des sciences opératoires. Elle conquiert, elle découvre quelque chose d'extraordinaire, on l'exploite et puis on laisse tomber.

La science est coloniale. Je parle de la science opératoire et non pas la connaissance pure. La science opératoire est coloniale.

Question: Je voudrais que vous parliez des frontières. Est-ce que ce n'est pas nécessaire de transgresser les frontières. C'est-à-dire d'oublier les proportions? Est-ce qu'on devrait toujours se rappeler de ces proportions, et si c'est le cas, est-ce qu'on est défini par les proportions?

Paul Virilio: Je crois qu'on ne peut pas entendre cette question sans dire évidemment oui. Mais ces proportions ne sont pas des frontières, ce sont des limites. C'est pour ça que la notion de limites est plus importante que celle des frontières. C'est pour cela que je dis que la frontière qui nous intéresse aujourd'hui, c'est l'horizon négatif. Ce n'est pas par hasard que les objets célestes ont des formes sphériques. Où est cette frontière négative? C'est la limite ou l'horizon négatif.

Question: Est-ce que les proportions sont une limite?

Paul Virilio: Les proportions sont la limite de l'être.

Question: Mais les proportions sont les relations?

Paul Virilio: Bien sûr comme la relativité et l'espace-temps, la vitesse n'est pas un phénomène, c'est la relation entre les phénomènes. C'est-à-dire qu'il y a des relations de proportions spatiales, la géométrie euclidienne et il y aussi les proportions temporaires, celles de la relativité et les phénomènes de l'accélération. On sent encore à quel point l'accélération de la réalité bouleverse tout y compris les phénomènes politiques. Les phénomènes démocratiques. L'accélération de l'histoire: L'accélération de la réalité, c'est-à-dire l'instantané, c'est l'attribut du divin. Un homme qui dispose de l'immédiat de l'ubiquité de l'instant, c'est celui qui peut réaliser un putsch médiatique.

Question: La manière de négocier les proportions à travers le désastre et à travers l'histoire ne marche plus à mon avis. Nous avons transcendé cette perspective et maintenant on a besoin de la technologie pour créer les désastres. Dans votre livre, la technologie créerait les désastres et que c'est la seule façon de faire revenir les proportions. Est-ce que c'est l'idée dont vous parliez dans Stratégies de la déception?

Paul Virilio: A côté de l'université, il y a l'arsenal. L'arsenal est l'académie du désastre. L'arsenal de Venise jusqu'à l'arsenal de Cherbourg ; on oublie que le musée de l'accident, le grand observatoire de la catastrophe, l'académie du désastre ça existe depuis l'arsenal de Venise. Dans les sciences opératoires, on a inventé les catastrophes jusqu'à la bombe atomique. Autrement dit, cette intelligence de la fin est déjà l'intelligence militaire. Simplement il faut arracher cette intelligence à la guerre pour faire face aux désastres. Que ça soit un désastre du complexe militaire industriel ou que ça soit un désastre de la finitude dont j'ai parlé tout à l'heure lié aux moyens de transport, lié à la transmission.

Einstein a dit qu'il y a trois bombes: la bombe atomique, la bombe informatique, et la bombe génétique de masse. L'abbé Pierre a rencontré Einstein. Ils ont discuté et Einstein lui a dit qu'il y a trois bombes. La bombe atomique tout le monde sait ce que c'était. La bombe informatique, s'il n'y a pas d'information le monde n'existe pas. Et la bombe démographique. On ne peut pas penser à la bombe démographique sans penser à la bombe génétique. Qui a le droit à la biotechnologie?

Question: J'ai une question sur la peur et ce que vous appelez la bombe informatique.

Paul Virilio: Je crois que l'université du désastre est évidement positive. C'est-à-dire qu'elle peut faire face à cette catastrophe de la finitude du progrès. Par tous les moyens. Il n'y a pas d'alternative contre la fin du progrès. Ce n'est pas que le progrès échoue, le progrès réussit et échoue dans la finitude.

A propos de la télésurveillance. Je veux juste faire une petite anecdote. Au moment de l'invention des chemins de fer anglais. Il y a un humoriste qui était aussi ingénieur qui disait que le grand problème dans l'emprise des chemins de fer c'est que ça marche dans les deux sens. La télésurveillance aussi.

Question: Est-ce que l'Arsenal n'est pas un lieu de pulsion de mort?

Paul Virilio: Oui, c'est un exemple mais on a aussi aujourd'hui un grand mal avec le kamikaze. Quelque part le kamikaze est une fuite de l'Arsenal. L'état suicidaire va d'un phénomène individuel à un phénomène collectif. C'est-à-dire que l'état suicidaire selon Lacan était un phénomène psychologique. Et il est devenu sociologique. D'où la multiplication extraordinaire de kamikazes en ce moment. Ce n'est pas le kamikaze c'est la démultiplication et la démesure du suicidaire. Quand on pense que c'est un terme qui est venu du japon, il ne faut pas oublier qu'il y a une contamination kamikaze japonaise sur les kamikazes proche orientaux. Le suicide actif n'est plus le suicide passif.

Même personne: oui, mais je crois qu'il y a quelque chose de différent entre ces deux genres de suicide. Pour le kamikaze, il y une origine culturelle alors que chez les kamikazes musulmans il y a quelque chose de plus relativiste.

Paul Virilio: Il y avait un moment très important dans l'empire du japon. Je m'intéresse beaucoup à ce qui s'est passé avant la bombe atomique, à un moment donné ils ont envisagé le suicide national. C'est-à-dire que par exemple, le premier signe du suicide national c'est que toute la flotte japonaise après Hiroshima, après Nagasaki, toute la flotte japonaise est allée se faire suicider et à ce moment là, il y a eu une réaction d'un soldat qui a dit « Nous, on ne peut pas suicider l'armée. Nous, on peut se suicider, c'est OK, mais si on suicide l'armée où va-t-on? » Il y avait plein de débats. Heureusement il y avait cette réflexion parce qu'ils avaient la tentation de passer du suicide individuel au suicide sociologique de masse, un suicide national. L'arsenal est avec la troisième intelligence. H. G. Wells a dit qu'il y a trois intelligences (humour anglais): l'intelligence animale, l'intelligence humaine, et l'intelligence militaire. La bombe atomique est liée au suicide.

Séance-II
la compression temporelle

Comme les peines d'accouchement, d'un affrontement, la compression temporelle de nos activités, de nos déplacements. provoque aujourd'hui une contraction des distances de délai qui est moins un signe d'une avancée positive que celui d'un nouveau type d'accident, d'un transfert de catastrophe écologique ne laissant pourtant aucune trace parce que la vitesse supersonique des transports aériens où l'instantanéité des télécommunications est toujours perçue comme un progrès incontestable.

La compression temporelle force pourtant de nous interroger sur la grave lacune d'une science écologique qui semble-t-il ne tire aucun compte du contrecoup de cette accélération. C'est une accélération cybernétique d'un temps réel qui conditionne et qui réduit finalement à rien la profondeur du champ de notre environnement et où la pollution de distance vient s'associer à cette pollution des substances qui concerne moins la nature des éléments que la grandeur nature, l'étendue du monde commun. En respectant les espaces de nos activités quotidiennes, on est en quelque sorte en train de parachever ceux de la biodiversité des espèces en voie de disparition. Cet événement relativiste a effectivement la matérialité du milieu humain. Son continuum spatio-temporel se pose pour nous après la question de l'accélération de l'histoire, de la réalité avec l'essor de l'interactivité désormais l'économie politique de nos sociétés développées. La faible grandeur nature de l'astre terrestre donne déjà de la peine à certains astronomes pour rechercher dans l'univers quelque planète exotique de substitution à celle trop étroite de nos origines.

Si la société de consommation devait s'étendre demain à toutes les nations non seulement notre veille terre périrait mais il en faudrait au moins trois pour satisfaire nos besoins. D'où cette quête sidérante d'une planète tellurique trois fois plus vaste que la nôtre. Donc, on constate que le séisme du progrès avec la contraction tellurique aussi bien que la distance du temp, est le signe avant-coureur d'une naissance à la fois espérée et redoutée dans la crainte d'une anormalité. Il y a la peur d'un handicap majeur qui résulterait de cette compression temporelle de la biosphère pour une humanité jadis née de son humus bien plus que de ses lointaines étoiles dont parlent si souvent nos astrophysiciens. Humain vient de humus et humus parle de l'humilité.

L'illusion lyrique d'un progrès soit disant grandissant mène à l'apparition conjointe des nanotechnologies de l'infiniment petit comme à la miniaturisation de l'infiniment grand de l'unique planète habitable du système solaire. Après l'annonce au siècle dernier de « la fin de l'histoire » du Fukuyama, il ne s'agit pas d'annoncer la fin de la géographie mais seulement d'évoquer le télescopage et l'accident d'un temps soit disant réel, qui ne tient nullement compte des limites sphériques de l'espace réel d'une petite planète en suspension provisoire pour la vie cosmique.

Question: Est-ce que ce discours vous mettra dans le camp de la décroissance?

Paul: Oui, certainement, sauf que je prends la décroissance au sens de décélération. Encore une fois, il ne s'agit pas de décroissance au niveau de la consommation. Je parlais de l'austérité sur l'état à propos de l'écologie. Non, je crois qu'il n'y aura pas de décroissance s'il n'y a pas une décélération. C'est-à-dire si on n'est pas conscient des phénomènes de production de la vitesse dans les domaines du transport et de la transmission.

Même personne: Oui, je parle de la thèse de la croissance économique.

Paul Virilio: Oui, là je vous dis depuis longtemps que je ne suis pas économiste. A côté de l'économie politique de la richesse, nous ne pouvons pas ne pas faire place à une économie politique de la vitesse. Richesse et vitesse sont liées. Accumulation et accélération sont liées. D'où une nouvelle intelligence de l'économie politique. Je rappelle que ce sont les physiocrates qui ont innové l'économie politique. Pas les économistes. Or, les écologistes sont des physiocrates à leur manière qui ont posé la question de l'économie politique de la vitesse. Et je crois que les problèmes énergétiques se posent actuellement, c'est-à-dire le problème de l'épuisement des ressources fossiles, etc., le problème du nucléaire. Je suis en train de vous dire que si on dit que le nucléaire serait idéal parce que ça ne pollue pas, et puis en plus il y en aura tant qu'on veut tandis que le charbon, le pétrole, il n'y en a plus, si on continue comme ça, au nom de l'écologie, on va carrément installer le nucléaire partout. Donc, on voit à quel point la politique énergétique ne peut pas exister aujourd'hui sans une économie politique et énergétique de la vitesse, de toutes les vitesses. Alors cela peut-être fait partie de la décroissance. Je parle de décélération. C'est dans l'ordre de la relativité du temps que je pose la question écologique et pas simplement dans le matérialisme des biens du capitalisme, etc.

En 1977 quand j'ai publié *Vitesse et Politique*, sur la quatrième de couverture j'ai mis cette phrase qui s'explique aujourd'hui. « La vitesse est la vieillesse du monde. » C'est capital. « La vitesse est la vieillesse du monde. » Si on prend au sérieux cette phrase, c'est-à-dire la contraction, j'ai 75 ans, pour vous dire que je ne suis pas aussi rigoureux que je l'ai été. Quelque part la vitesse m'a vieilli. La vitesse de la vie, parce que la vie, c'est la vitesse. Je suis vif ou moins vif. Vif, vitesse, pareil. Il faut comprendre que nous faisons vieillir le monde par les phénomènes d'accélération de la réalité. D'où l'économie politique de la vitesse.

Wolfgang Schirmacher: Tu parles de la vie et la vitesse du monde extérieur. Mais est-ce qu'on ne peut pas avoir une vie intérieure qui devient de plus en plus rigoureuse due à la sagesse atteinte: Rilke parle d'une foi intérieure.

Paul Virilio: Je ne fais pas trop de distinction entre l'extérieur et l'intérieur. Contrairement à mon ancien ami Jean Baudrillard, je n'ai aucune culture psychanalytique. Zéro, cela ne m'intéresse pas. Ceci dit. Je suis tout à fait conscient que cet accident de la réalité, l'accélération de la réalité et non pas simplement de l'histoire est une occasion inouïe de développement de la connaissance. Derrière chaque accident, derrière chaque catastrophe, et à plus forte raison derrière l'accident intégral de connaissance, il y a une énorme espérance d'un nouveau savoir. Le savoir lié à la grandeur de la petitesse, lié à la grandeur de l'humilité, a la grandeur de l'échec. Je crois que l'université Européenne, elle s'est fondée contre la barbarie, au sens large. Je ne vais pas rentrer dans les détails. Contre la barbarie, l'université est née autour de l'an 1000 à Bologne, Rome, etc. Je crois que aujourd'hui, la nouvelle université, celle du désastre- fait face non pas à la barbarie, mais à cet énorme catastrophe qu'est la méduse du progrès. Le progrès est une sorte de méduse qu'il faut regarder en face avec un miroir. Donc, je suis d'accord avec vous, qu'il y a une chance inouïe. D'ailleurs, je n'écrirais pas ce j'ai écrit si j'étais désespéré. Je n'écrirais pas. Je ne sais pas ce que je ferais, mais vous voyez ce que je veux dire.

Wolfgang Schirmacher: Je suis d'accord avec la dernière phrase. (Le progrès est une sorte de méduse, qu'il faut regarder en face avec un miroir.) Parce que quand je parle du savoir, je ne parle pas de savoir scientifique. Je parle de la connaissance socratique: connaissez vous-même. Qui suis-je? Est-ce que je suis mes voyages? Est-ce que je suis mes spéculations sur les autres planètes? Ou est-ce je suis l'être qui peut passer 3 heures en train d'écouter et de réfléchir. D'avoir une vie innée. Jean Baudrillard, vous savez son annonce de décès (qu'il a écrit lui-même) disait que « L'existence n'est pas tout. C'est même la moindre des choses. »

Paul Virilio: Par rapport à Baudrillard, il n'y avait pas « grand chose pour » s'entendre. Comme dit l'autre, on n'a pas besoin d'être d'accord pour s'entendre, et Jean, c'est un très grand ami. Sur beaucoup de points je n'étais absolument pas d'accord. Bon, vous avez compris que je suis chrétien. C'est-à-dire que je ne crois pas à la mort, lui ne croyait pas à la vie. C'est-à-dire à la réalité de la vie. D'où la simulation, etc. Tous les deux nous étions des objecteurs de conscience. Des athées, mais pas les mêmes. Lui ne croyait pas à la réalité, en particulier a son accélération, et moi, je ne crois pas à la mort, c'est-à-dire à la cessation.

Je dis dans mon prochaine livre que l'accident intégral a une dimension « apocalyptique ». Je rappelle que l'apocalypse veut dire la révélation. L'accident intégral est une révélation. La finitude du monde et non pas la fin du monde. La fin, on s'en fout, il n'y aucun intérêt. La finitude du monde, c'est une révélation, et elle va l'être de plus en plus. La révélation selon moi, se pose contre la révolution. Quand quelqu'un me demande, tu es quoi, tu es un révolutionnaire. Je dis non, je suis un *révélationnaire*. Et oui ! Je le crois profondément. Je ne suis pas apocalyptique. Je le répète, la fin du monde est un concept sans avenir. Il n'y aucun intérêt dans la fin du monde. « Le boom », il n'y aura plus rien, ça n'a aucun intérêt pour un intellectuel ou un penseur. La fin du monde, c'est zéro. Baudrillard était d'accord, la fin du monde, c'est un concept sans avenir. Bon, par contre, *révélationnaire*. Oui, je suis *révélationnaire*. Pas simplement au niveau de la foi, mais au niveau de mon travail. Ce n'est pas tout à fait pareil. L'écologie grise est *révélationnaire*. La révolution participait d'une cosmogonie, pas simplement parce que elle fait référence à la révolution astronomique, mais parce qu'elle a entrainé la révolution idéologique. Et on sait bien qu'ils ont échoué. Ceux qui attendent encore la révolution se sont trompés de planète. Moi, j'attends la révélation. Quand je dis je l'attends c'est une façon de parler parce que j'essaie de travailler avec cette révélation, ce qui n'est pas la fin mais la finitude. C'est à dire qu'il nous ouvre une nouvelle pensée : la grandeur de la minceur. « D'ultra-mince » comme dirait Marcel Duchamp.

Je suis désolé que mes gestes ne passent pas d'une langue à
une autre. Vous savez il y a un homme qui travaillait
beaucoup sur la pauvreté: Léautaud? C'est un homme
intéressant. Au moment de sa mort, quelqu'un lui demandait
que ressens-tu? Il disait une immense curiosité. Moi aussi. Je
ne parle pas de la mort, la fin, mais de la finitude. Une
immense curiosité devant la finitude. Devant la révélation de
la finitude. Parce qu'elle va concerner la philosophie,
l'économie, l'astrophysique si orgueilleuse, dont celle
Monsieur Stephen Hawking si intelligent. Je crois qu'il y a
aussi des accidents scientifiques qui se préparent. Beaucoup
commencent à se poser des questions sur l'espace et le temps.
Dans son dernier livre, Martin Rees, l'astrophysicien qui
étudie les tremblements de terre disait que la science moderne
s'intéressait à la matière. Nous, il va falloir s'intéresser à la
nature de l'espace et du temps. Je suis tout à fait d'accord avec
lui. C'est là où la révélation est possible. Une immense
curiosité. L'université du désastre c'est ça, c'est-à-dire, de
faire face à cette révélation-là, qui est au-delà de la révélation
copernicienne, qui est au-delà de Galilée. Ce qui nous
concerne, c'est l'intérieur et l'extérieur de la pensée donc qui
refont l'université non pas sur le désastre de la barbarie, mais
sur le désastre du savoir que la finitude va imposer. Le
désastre de la pensée impose une nouvelle pensée. Ça me
dépasse infiniment et c'est ça qui m'excite beaucoup. Ça me
dépasse. Dans le nord du Canada il y a des Inuits. Nous, je
dirais que nous devrions tous devenir les inouïes. (Face à
l'accident intégral.)

J'espère que cela relancera la philosophie, puisque je la trouve
pas mal accidentée. Depuis la mort de Deleuze et de tous ces
gens-là, la philosophie est en panne à mon avis. C'est pour ça
qu'on parle d'Aristote, ou Platon. On revient aux Grecs. Moi,
je les ai tous connus, je dirai que la philosophie n'est pas très
brillante en ce moment. On est des phénoménologues, et puis
on est revenu à la phénoménologie de Merleau-Ponty, etc.
Quand j'ai fait mon premier séminaire à Barcelone, au Collège
International de Philosophie, il y avait un grand débat sur
Heidegger et le nazisme. Moi je leur ai dit, je vous préviens, je

suis husserlien. Je ne suis pas heideggérien. J'aime bien Heidegger, mais je suis Husserlien. Je suis phénoménologue. Un dromologue est forcément un phénoménologue. Et je crois qu'aujourd'hui, le retour à la phénoménologie c'est un sacré signe de la panne philosophique du 20eme siècle. Si vous voyez l'impact de Hannah Arendt, ou Edith Stein.

Question: La série, « L'espace critique » que vous avez crée avec Georges Perec, je crois. Je pense à Perec qui utilise certaines règles comme écrire un livre sans la lettre E etc. Est-ce que son écriture est un exemple dans la littérature ou une écriture pour concevoir ce que vous dites concernant l'accident intégral?

Paul Virilio: Oui, je le crois, aussi. Mais il ne faut pas séparer la littérature de la remise en cause géométrique par Mandelbrot. J'ai été un des premiers à écrire sur Mandelbrot dans ma revue critique. Je me souviens, il y avait un numéro spécial sur les maths et un ami m'a demandé si je voulais faire quelque chose. Je lui ai dit que les maths n'étaient pas mon truc et puis je tombe sur la première édition sur la géométrie fractale, les objets fractals de Mandelbrot, je tombe là-dedans et je trouve ça extraordinaire. Et puis, Mandelbrot est venu à mon cours. Et puis, je revois Jean-Pierre et je lui dis, j'ai quelqu'un, il faut que vous parliez sur les maths, Mandelbrot. On a parlé de beaucoup de choses, mais on n'a pas parlé de l'accident intégral. Mandelbrot était mal reçu en France, c'est pour ça qu'il est partie aux États-Unis, et quand il revient en France, il n'était pas très content, parce qu'il n'était pas reçu. Donc, c'est vrai que d'un côté on a les dérives pereciennes et je l'accompagne, moi aussi, je suis un homme de la ville, comme dirait Edgar Poe, un homme de la foule : celui qui défile, qui dérive. Le piétonne de Paris, le Rétife de la Bretonne. Tout ça fait partie de mon intelligence de l'espace urbain, et donc avec Perec, on dirait qu'on délirait ensemble et donc, il y avait effectivement une dimension littéraire en commun. Ce premier livre que j'ai publié c'était *Espèce d'espace* et à partir de la, j'ai découvert chez Mandelbrot et ailleurs, qu'il y avait des géométries qui participaient à la même logique fractionnaire. Les dimensions entières n'étaient plus une pierre. Elles étaient fractionnées, accidentées, pulvérisées, et cette pulvérisation de la géométrie qui m'a effectivement renseigné sur la vitesse, m'a beaucoup inspiré dans ma recherche qui s'appelle « de l'espace critique ». Le mot *infra-ordinaire,* c'est un mot qu'on a forgé ensemble et puis il l'a repris.

Question: Est-ce qu'il y a une écriture qui est propre à l'accident? Un style?

Paul Virilio: Oui, mais l'accident est tellement une grande question. Comment dire.

On est obligé de faire référence au titre d'un très grand livre de Blanchot, c'est-à-dire *L'écriture du Désastre.* Et effectivement l'exposition que j'ai organisée à la fondation Cartier, en 2003, pour étudier l'accident, le désastre etc., était une tentative d'entrer dans cette écriture la. Mais cela me dépasse infiniment. Ceci dit, c'est vrai qu'il y un langage de la catastrophe, une écriture du désastre. Mais cette écriture se révélera dans l'université du désastre au croisement de toutes les disciplines. Ce n'est pas seulement un phénomène poétique ou littéraire. C'est un phénomène scientifique aussi. Quelque part elle a été traitée dans l'arsenal. L'écriture du désastre, c'est l'écriture de la stratégie et de la tactique, c'est l'écriture de la guerre totale. C'est l'écriture du kamikaze dont on parlait a la fin de la matinée. L'écriture du désastre c'est celle de guerre, c'est l'intelligence militaire. Je la connais bien je suis un enfant de la guerre. Donc, l'écriture du désastre je l'ai apprise à la guerre pendant les bombardements de Nantes. Pour moi, le désastre, c'est celui de l'invention de la guerre moderne. La guerre ancienne, la guerre civile, les tumultes des origines sont les grandes bagarres. Même s'il y a beaucoup de morts, ce sont les grandes bagarres. On oublie vite que le stratège n'est pas seulement la mère de la ville grecque, mais c'est celui qui va penser l'écriture du désastre de l'autre sans penser que ce désastre de l'autre est aussi le sien. Donc, il y a une intelligence militaire effectivement et là, ce n'est pas une blague, une intelligence militaire qu'il faut détourner, on est obligé de la détourner de son extermination par la finitude du monde. Et quand je vois le dernier texte paru au Monde de Kissinger, qu'il faut dénucléariser la planète. Quand on a suivi la pensée de Kissinger et de l'Amérique de cette époque là, de la guerre froide, c'est vraiment une révélation. C'est une révélation qui donne raison à un grand spécialiste de la logistique qui s'appelait Dwight Eisenhower. C'est-à-dire qu'il était conscient de la finitude. C'est-à-dire de l'approvisionnement en pétrole, approvisionnement en munition et en image à travers la connaissance aérienne etc. Donc, pour moi, si je suis entré en plain-pied dans la catastrophe, c'est parce que je suis un enfant de cette catastrophe. J'ai souvent dit que la guerre a été mon père et ma mère. La destruction des villes pendant la seconde guerre mondiale a été mon université. Oui, il y a une écriture du désastre et il est écrit dans tous les arsenaux. Les arsenaux comme j'ai dit sont les académies du désastre.

Ce que je dis là est rude. C'est très difficile d'être rude aujourd'hui. Il y a une dimension réellement tragique dans l'état du monde, or, notre société est fondée sur la tragédie, la tragédie grec, elle est fondatrice de l'occident. Quelque part cette pensée du tragique est toujours très mal vue. Or, non, nous sommes devant un retour du tragique. Comme à l'origine de l'histoire occidentale, comme à l'origine d'Antigone, Oedipe, etc. Il y a un retour du tragique, et ce retour n'est pas simplement dans la littérature, il est dans la philo, dans la science, dans la politique, il est partout. Donc, au cours de la modernité, l'intelligence militaire dont on parlait tout à l'heure, elle a militarisé la science. L'arsenal a totalement militarisé la science, et en particulier à partir bien sûr du nucléaire et tout qui a suivi. Or, l'intelligence du désastre, la révélation dont on a parlé toute à l'heure, doit civiliser, ré-civiliser cette science, c'est-à-dire la mettre face à sa dimension exterminatrice. C'est dans ce sens que c'était un grand projet universitaire au début de l'an 2000. Pas comme le début de l'an 1000, il s'agissait de lutter contre les barbaries. Aujourd'hui la barbarie c'est la barbarie de notre succès.

Quelque part l'idée de la paix universelle, elle revient, face à l'extermination définitive. La destruction massive est effectivement la question de la fonction politique de guerre. Ils mettent un terme à l'histoire et à la géographie. C'est évidement une grande question écologique. C'est-à-dire le suicide national deviendra le suicide international, mondial. C'est-à-dire on s'inspirait du japon d'Hirohito, en osant l'idée d'un suicide mondial, global. La question de la paix universelle, ça ne veut pas dire la paix au sens « tout va bien », ça veut dire que le principe même de l'art de la guerre est remis en cause comme la science est remise en cause. La finitude remet en cause l'art de la guerre comme l'art politique, comme l'art de la philosophie. Là, il y a une révélation qui met fin à l'histoire de l'art de la guerre. D'où d'ailleurs un terme nouveau qui m'intéresse beaucoup, de dissuasion. Ils nous ont parlé de la dissuasion pendant la guerre froide beaucoup. Aujourd'hui la dissuasion vient de cette situation, on a des clips. Ce n'est plus une arme qui nous dissuade, c'est la finitude qui nous dissuade. Ce n'est plus le rouge et le bleu et le blanc avec des fusées qui disent que si tu fais ceci je t'en envois les balistiques et machin. C'est la finitude même qui dissuade la pensée de la guerre et la pensée de la science qui mène à la guerre. Et là, il y a quelque chose d'inouïe qui me dépasse totalement, on sait rien. Et je suis fier de ne pas savoir. Parce que si je vous disais que je sais comme tellement de gens disent à ce moment : « On a compris la localisation » c'est non, parce que on n'a pas compris la finitude écologique.

Question: Est-ce que tout ça implique aussi l'empathie?

Paul Virilio: Oui, certainement. Bien sûr, c'est un terme, que j'aime bien, et c'est de quoi il ne s'agit point. Mais comment dire? Là, où on trouve la phénoménologie, on trouve la déception. C'est-à-dire, on rentre dans la perception des événements, et les perceptions des événements, c'est l'autre, c'est le milieu, et là il y a un énorme travail à faire, parce que nous sommes victimes, je dirais, de la télé-objectivité. L'empathie, c'est-à-dire, la perception d'autrui, la perception du monde, elle est liée à l'objectivité, la subjectivité, or nous avons inventé les technologies, avec quelques exceptions, qui idole la télé-objectivité. Là encore le temps réel est déterminant: Google Earth, la télésurveillance, etc. Donc, on est devant un phénomène de pathologie de la perception. Il y a une maladie, je ne sais pas comment dire en anglais, le glaucome. C'est-à-dire sans le savoir, on souffre d'une restriction du spectre visuel et on perd la latéralité. C'est exactement ce qui se passe dans l'écran. La télé-objectivité est un glaucome qui pourra mettre en cause l'empathie. L'empathie est la tête du champ visuel intégral. Dans la vie ici, maintenant, dans la perception divine, et non pas par le truchement d'un écran, d'un télescope, d'un microscope, ou d'un écran de télé. Là, il y a un élément très important. Je suis étonné à quel point aujourd'hui, ce n'est pas seulement à cause du téléphone portable, ce n'est pas seulement à cause de l'ordinateur, à quel point, les gens ne s'orientent plus dans la vie. Ils ont perdu la perception de leur environnement latérale. Ils ne sont pas conscients de ce glaucome de l'écran, de l'ubiquité de l'écran. Dans le phénomène d'orientation, la latéralisation est déterminante. On sait bien que quand on vise une cible, on perd le champ. Là, aujourd'hui, la cible, c'est nous, et quelque part, nous perdons le champ latéral. Dans la relation interpersonnelle, c'est déterminant. Dans les relations entre l'environnement et l'espace, c'est déterminant. Mais je crois que le mot empathie, je pense à Klee, vous avez raison, va être un mot qui revient de plus en plus. Il y a un livre très intéressant, de comment s'appelle-t-il, *Abstraktion und Einfuhlung* de Wilhelm Worringer, il faut le lire, qui montre la relation qui existe entre l'empathie et l'abstraction. Parce que la perte d'empathie mène à l'abstraction. L'écran mène à l'abstraction. Ce livre de Worringer m'a beaucoup inspiré. Je suis un vieux gestaltiste. La psychologie de formes m'a passionné. Je ne crois pas aux formes, bien sur que non, mais la psychologie des formes m'a inspiré, toute l'école de Mach, c'était les années 50-60, m'a inspiré et Worringer, c'est son travail qui l'ouvre.

Question: Si on perd l'empathie avec l'abstraction, qu'est ce qu'on gagne?

Paul Virilio: Je crois que si je prends l'art contemporain, l'abstraction ne nous a pas beaucoup apporté. J'ai connu beaucoup de peintres, j'ai connu pratiquement tous les peintres, Matisse, bon, je ne peux pas tout réciter. J'étais de ce milieu-là quand j'étais très jeune. Donc, la querelle, qui a pas mal agité la peinture, en particulier autour Nicolas de Staël qui parlait des gangs d'abstraction à fond, un terme que j'ai bien aimé, à l'époque où on parlait des gangs d'action contre l'assurance des voitures Citroën et lui qui disait qu'il avait une sorte de gang d'abstraction. C'est vrai que c'était une chose qui m'a beaucoup intéressé. Ceci dit, l'abstraction a posé la question du visible et de l'invisible, peut-être la grande question d'après-guerre. D'après-guerre dans la question de l'art, c'est que l'invisible devient visible, c'est la tabula rasa. C'est Auschwitz et Hiroshima. Moi-même, j'ai été touché par cette abstraction qui était un événement de ma jeunesse. Quand Nantes a été bombardé, je vous donne un exemple. Pour un enfant, une ville c'est comme des Alpes. Quand on voit l'après-midi en quelques instants, on voit la maison et tout est écrasé. On ne peut plus le voir. On devient des objecteurs de conscience. On n'y croit plus. Si seulement je comprenais que l'éternel puisse disparaître en un clin d'œil, etc. Donc, l'abstraction est liée à l'anticipation de cette destruction et à la succession, de ce qui s'est passé. Là encore, l'abstraction est liée à la guerre. On ne peut pas comprendre l'abstraction, le néo-expressionnisme, sans la Première et Deuxième guerre mondiale. De même avec la surveillance.

Hubertus von Amelunxen: Ayant pratiquement lu tout ce que tu as publié, je n'ai jamais compris L'art à perte du vue *parce que tu prends ce qui a été l'argument fondateur du modernisme, de rendre visible, et tu le retournes en disant que l'abstraction anticipe le devenir invisible du visible.*

Paul Virilio: Exactement. C'était vraiment un moment historique, c'est pour ça que j'aimais l'abstraction tout en étant un homme de la figuration.

Hubertus von Amelunxen: Je suis beaucoup plus d'accord avec toi maintenant. Il faut qu'on en parle plus.

Paul Virilio: D'autant plus que la première machine de vitesse n'est pas la locomotive de la révolution industrielle mais l'appareil photographique. La machine de vitesse, c'est la machine de vision. C'est l'instantanéité. Vous voyez l'hystérie sur l'invention de l'instantanéité, c'est fabuleux. Autrement dit, le monde a été révolutionné, par l'appareil photo bien plus que par la machine à vapeur ou par la locomotive, ou par le TGV, etc. Et là, cette logique aujourd'hui de la photographie, on en parlera demain, crée une valeur incomparable à celle de l'art, elle a anticipé tous les phénomènes qu'on a traités depuis, Nevers et jusqu'à Lord Snowdon dont je parle dans mon dernier livre. Il était le photographe de la cour d'Angleterre, un ancien mari de la Margaret, qui a dit que la photo n'est pas d'art ; c'est de la spontanéité. Donc, quelque part là, l'appareil photo est un objet bien plus emblématique que tous ce qu'on a décrit, que les moteurs les plus rapides, etc.

Hubertus von Amelunxen: Nous allons parler à propos de tout ça plus tard, mais je voulais parler de Rodolphe Toepffer qui disait en 1841, que la photographie était la diminution du monde parce que ça nous apporterait le lointain et que dans ce sens ça détruirait tout le fantasme du lointain dont on a besoin pour construire notre présent à venir.

Paul Virilio: C'est la machine originelle d'accélération, de la vitesse c'est l'appareil photo. Je sais quand j'ai fait une étude sur la vitesse à la Fondation Cartier, j'ai mis trop de véhicules. Je voulais avec ces véhicules, exposer ce que je viens de dire avec les Ferrari, les jets, etc. J'ai eu la chance de confondre le temps du cinéma avec le temps réel, dans une des maisons du cinéma. Il y avait d'ailleurs un local sonore qui a bien servi à contrarier les forces anti-aériennes pendant l'occupation. J'ai demandé qu'on mette une diffusion de la parabole pour avoir le temps réel des informations. On avait le programme qui s'appelait « le bon plaisir de Paul Virilio » et qui durait 2 heures, et pendant ce « bon plaisir », dans cette pièce où on avait les informations continues du monde, on a eu le putsch d'Eltsine, la fin de Gorbatchev en direct, et là j'étais très heureux parce que au moins on avait cet accident. Depuis j'ai reçu une lettre de Gorbatchev. J'étais très fier.

Wolfgang Schirmacher: Qu'est ce que c'est exactement ton objectif? Pourquoi toujours discuter des choses en termes du placement et de la distinction, kaputt! Pourquoi ne pas dire que c'est bien d'avoir les deux: media universel, les artistes et aussi l'idée de Baudrillard? Pourquoi devrait-on choisir entre une façon de percevoir et une autre? Pourquoi est-ce qu'on ne peut pas avoir tant qu'on veut? Qui dit qu'on ne peut pas être fort? Qui dit que quand on est né, l'autre sera mort? Ça changera. L'effort pour changer le monde avec la création de la photographie a enrichi le monde.

Paul Virilio: Il a fait les deux en même temps. C'est la catastrophe de son succès. Le succès est une catastrophe en même temps. Vous savez la phrase d'Hannah Arendt, « Le progrès et la catastrophe sont l'envers et le revers de la même médaille. »

Wolfgang Schirmacher: Mon ami et ton ami aussi, Lyotard, était intelligent de ne pas attaquer le progrès, il a utilisé le mot « développement ». Le développement est ouvert. Ça ne devrait pas être le progrès, mais c'est le changement qui est reconnu malgré ce qui se passe. J'étais d'accord et j'ai compris par cet idée que dans la vie quotidienne, les différentes formes de média ont une tendance de remplacer les choses, les gens n'ont pas le temps de grandir avec les média. Les gens ont besoin de travailler. Mais dans notre travail ici, nous sommes des gens avec des esprits d'artiste. Pour nous, chaque perception nouvelle, chaque façon neuve de voir les choses, de les découvrir est bien. Nous n'avons pas de mal à avoir mille modes de perception. Cela ne veut pas dire que la perception est perdue, c'est gagné. Il y a un changement. Avec ton discours, ce qui me pose un problème, c'est où est la bonne nouvelle?

Où se trouvent « les bonnes nouvelles »? Où est la nouvelle constructive? Je suis d'accord avec toutes tes critiques mais une crise est aussi une opportunité. Il y a quelque chose d'autre qui se passe. Les humains seront capables d'être plus qu'humain, super-humain si vous voulez. Nietzsche— Übermensch.

Paul Virilio: On revient toujours à la question de « ma » négativité. Alors qu'en réalité, je ne suis pas tout négatif. Je pense simplement qu'on est en train de découvrir une nouvelle dimension de la science, et de la connaissance. Et je crois que c'est ça, la révélation. C'est que la limite va au-delà de la limite. Elle nous fait prendre conscience que l'environnement est beaucoup plus qu'un environnement géographique et physique, c'est un environnement philosophique. Je connais, je reconnais bien dans cette question des choses qui me travaillent personnellement. Virilio est catastrophique. Virilio est négatif. Si vous voulez, mais c'est faux. Ce qui m'intéresse, c'est d'aller au-delà de la méduse. C'est de ne pas détourner le regard de la méduse. C'est justement de faire face à cette catastrophe. Tous ce que vous dites, non seulement, je l'admets, je n'ai rien d'autre à dire. Je ne suis pas en train de pleurer sur le progrès. Je ne suis pas en train de pleurer sur le malheur du monde. Je suis profondément excité par cette catastrophe. C'est ça, être un révélationnaire. C'est de ne pas détourner le regard de la négativité. C'est de regarder la négativité avec un miroir. Je sais les raisons que vous avez de dire tout ça, mais comment dire. Si vous me permettez, je suis un peu fatigué de ce ping-pong. C'est-à-dire, du renvoi de la balle. « Oui, mais si vous dites ça, ça veut dire que. » Non, ça ne veut pas dire ça. Ce que je dis me dépasse. Et ça m'excite d'être dépassé dans cette pensée. Et en ce sens, vous avez tout à fait raison. La catastrophe de la photographie, elle est une merveille, je ne veux pas supprimer les appareils photographiques. Ce que je dis c'est que la limite et la finitude sont au cœur de notre histoire. Alors, vous l'appelez le développement ou le progrès, peu importe. La limite est là. Et la manière de dire, ça peut-être ceci ou cela, est de ne pas regarder en face la méduse. Si tous vous êtes là, je suis très heureux. C'est vous qui venez d'ailleurs. Vous n'êtes pas Français. Si vous savez comment je suis emmerdé par les Français. Et oui, c'est pour ça que je suis heureux que vous soyez là et vous disiez tous ce que vous dites. Mais ce que je viens d'entendre me rappelle ce que disent les français. La raison pour laquelle j'ai accepté de faire ce cours pendant ce festival, pour ne par dire séminaire, parce que le seul honneur que j'ai, c'est vous. C'est vous d'ailleurs. Vous des antipodes. Vous d'ailleurs. Je tiens de vous dire, parce que si je suis à La Rochelle, c'est que quelque part j'ai déserté Paris et les vagues de la victoire parisienne qui ne mène n'a rien.

Je voudrais dire, parce que c'est tellement important, est que ça me dépasse, que le statut d'objection philosophique lui-même est éteint. Le débat contre la victoire est éteint par cette finitude. L'extermination remet en cause le dialogue philosophique sous ses formes anciennes. Non pas pour contrarier l'objection et demander un assentiment parfait, ça sera absolument emmerdant. Je suis à moitié italien moi, j'ai du plaisir à ça. J'ai du plaisir dans le sport intellectuel. Mais, je crois que le statut d'objection est à reconstruire totalement. Comment poser l'objection devant cette situation? Comment déplacer la disputatio/disputatio? En France, je peux vous dire, c'est paralysé. Depuis les années 60 où on a eu la grande liberté des sixties et Deleuze, Lyotard, et Guattari, on était sortis de l'objection cartésienne. Et tout ça s'est éteint et là, aujourd'hui c'est fini. On est revenu en arrière, on est revenu sur la veille disputatio. C'est pour ça que je tiens peu à mes relations avec les philosophes. On n'est pas face à la catastrophe, on est en face de la finitude. On n'a pas trouvé le moyen d'échanger la contradiction. Il va falloir inventer un nouveau rapport à la contradiction et à l'objection. C'est, à mon avis, la question philosophique majeure, en particulier en

France, parce qu'en France, là c'est terrible. Vous savez d'ailleurs, comme moi. Encore, une expression, « il faut rire » parce que comme disait Lacan, si ça ne rit pas, ça ne communique pas. C'est pour ça que je disais ce matin à propos de Baudrillard, on n'a pas besoin d'être d'accord pour s'entendre. En France, on a absolument besoin d'être d'accord pour s'entendre. Hier comprendre, était l'art des arts. Aujourd'hui, il faut deviner. Ça change honnêtement le statut du dialogue. C'est très important à mon avis.

Question: Concernant un cas qu'on peut voir comme une façon de répondre à cette situation.

Paul Virilio: Comme je disais auparavant, je n'ai pas raison. Je ne peux pas avoir raison aujourd'hui parce que la question est *open*. La limite, la finitude est une situation d'ouverture qui excède la pensée philosophique, la pensée politique aujourd'hui. Donc, la mienne. C'est pour ça que le débat en France sur la raison, la raison cartésienne, etc., est totalement ringard. Totalement dépassé. La phrase de notre génération: Comment adhérer à quelque chose comme ça? Par exemple, « il faut deviner la finitude du monde », on ne le comprend pas. On en comprendra dans « x » génération quand on aura abordé la finitude. C'est la révélation de la fin du monde, du monde fini. Oui, il y a un dépassement du concept traditionnel de la raison, du raisonnement qui va nous lancer dans le délire de n'importe quoi. Mais du travail des philosophes des années 60, je pense qui pourrait apparaître délirant, je pense à Guattari, etc.: Est-ce qu'il *connait* une réponse à la situation du dépassement de la raison et le raisonnement du statut traditionnel de dialogue et de l'objection, etc.? La situation est *open*. En ce moment, on lance des accords « open sky » pour les transports transatlantiques, vous savez, mais ce qui est « open » est exactement la question de la finitude. Elle (la question de la finitude) dépasse notre compréhension, notre art de comprendre, et avec laquelle on a construit deux mille ans de l'histoire. C'est ça aussi la crise de l'université. Elle est l'héritière depuis l'an mille, elle est l'héritière de cette construction du dialogue de la contradiction d'objection a travers ces différents pensées. On est devant un événement considérable. L'accident de la connaissance, l'accident de la compréhension traditionnelle, je dirais, est un événement considérable qui nous excède, si vous êtes prêt avec moi à entrer dans cet excès la, nous pouvons continuer à dialoguer. Si pour des raisons traditionnelles, vous refermez la question de la contradiction et de débats traditionnelles, nous ne pouvons pas avancer, avancer dans ce monde ouvert de la fin. Le monde de la fin, de la finitude, est un monde ouvert pour la pensée, pour la science. C'est ça l'accident de la science. L'accident de la connaissance est un événement sans pareil. C'est un élément sans référence. L'accident de la substance, on a chez Aristote, etc. L'accident de la connaissance que j'essaie de vous dire avec des mots malheureux qui ne sont pas à la hauteur. Ils me vantent. Si je vous ai dit que j'ai raison, ça serait absurde, tout que j'ai dit serait absurde. C'est ça la grandeur de pauvreté. Il y a une telle puissance, une telle révélation qu'on ne peut pas être à la hauteur.

Séance-III
L'art à perte de vue

Après ce que notre ami venait de dire, on peut comprendre la
phrase de Stockhausen disant que le grand chef-d'œuvre de
l'histoire c'est le ground zéro. Trois mille corps qui
disparaissent, c'est logique. Et ensuite ça tourne sur la
télévision en boucle. Ça tourne pour toujours et partout. C'est
le chef-d'œuvre de la mort. La chute des corps.

Je veux commencer d'abord avec une petite introduction par
rapport au dialogue que nous avons eu hier avec Wolfgang
(Schirmacher). Parce que ça m'a ouvert l'esprit sur quelque
chose que je développerai ultérieurement: pourquoi c'est utile,
le dialogue et la disputatio. Aujourd'hui le statut de
l'objection, de la critique, de la disputation, changent. On ne
dialogue pas. On ne débat pas de la même manière dans un
canot de sauvetage, dans un amphithéâtre, ou une salle de
cours. Vous voyez déjà, la modification du débat à la télé,
avec la rapidité des échanges. Elle bouleverse le contenu du
dialogue entre le présentateur si bien nommé et son invité.
C'est ce que j'appelle le « ping-pong ». « Vous avez cinq
secondes pour répondre. » « Ping-pong ». Le caractère limité
dans le temps de la situation présent conditionne le contenu du
dialogue. Quand je regarde la télévision, j'ai horreur de ça. Je
suis Italien, j'ai du temps pour parler.

Après ce qu'on a appelé la phénoménologie empathique, qui a
ouvert le dialogue, la dramaturgie arrive et impose sa
contrainte antipathique. On va parler de l'art : deux aspects, la
guerre et évidement l'instantanéité. Deux aspects qui
conditionnent la perte du point de vue artistique. La Guerre, la
Première, mondaine. La Deuxième, totale. Pas du tout pareille.
Cette guerre, elle va conditionner l'art et la culture occidentale
intégralement. L'art, la culture occidentale a été une victime
de guerre. La question c'est: est-elle invalide ou est-elle
invalidée? Je crois que c'est très important, parce que l'art a

une dimension qui triomphe de la critique. La première phase de l'impressionnisme relativiste, plus que le cubisme, introduisait la relativité Einsteinienne à l'expressionnisme, Otto Dix et tous les expressionnistes. Qu'est ce qui s'est passé entre les guerres? La commune de Paris, la guerre de 1870, la guerre de 1914 et la Deuxième Guerre. L'expressionnisme est venu après la Première Guerre mondiale. C'est la première blessure, le premier handicap de l'art. Ensuite, nous avons eu le surréalisme. On ne peut pas comprendre le surréalisme, « les champs magnétiques », Breton, Aragon, sans la merveille des feux d'artifices de la guerre. Les explosions, les gaz, etc. Et après la Seconde Guerre mondiale, on a eu l'activisme dont on ne parle pas assez. On ne peut pas comprendre l'art d'aujourd'hui sans l'activisme viennois. Et tout ça bien sûr, en passant par l'abstraction, la perte de vue déjà de la figure, la non-figuration du stand-in et la déportation de l'art. Je répète que la Première Guerre mondiale était marquée par la déportation des populations, mais aussi par la déportation de l'art de l'Europe en Amérique. C'était un événement de guerre. On ne peut pas comprendre le transfert de l'art européen, qui était l'avant-garde, vers l'art américain appelé « contemporain » sans la déportation de guerre. On a déporté des juives, on a déporté l'art. Pourquoi est-qu'on n'en parle plus? Un autre aspect qui conditionne la perte du point de vue de l'art, c'est devant la vitesse, devant l'instantanéité. J'ai dit hier la photographie, l'instantanéité de la photographie, puis cinématographie, et enfin devenant réelle à travers la télé, avec l'impérialisme du temps réel médiatisé, l'art contemporain est devenu moins contemporain que fatalement intemporain. Le mot est important. Contre l'art contemporain, il y a l'art intemporain. C'est-à-dire qu'il a rompu avec ses filiations historiques. L'art contemporain est en rupture accidentelle avec les origines de l'art. Je vais lire un petit extrait dans mon livre, parce que ça le résume très bien. Au début de l'année 2007, le directeur du musée de l'art contemporain à Vienne m'a demandé d'écrire un petit texte sur l'art, un poche sur le programme de l'année à venir et je vous donne un petit extrait.

« Au 19ème siècle avec l'impressionnisme et sa phénoménologie, c'était la liberté d'impression qui était délivrée de l'académisme. Au 20ème siècle avec l'expressionnisme et sa dramaturgie, c'était la liberté d'expression qui s'était libérée de toute sorte de conformisme. Au 21ème, au quotidien, ces deux libertés de l'esprit sont menacées de disparaître devant l'accélération d'une réalité numérique qui efface jusqu'aux souvenirs de toute représentation. Face à cela, le musée d'art contemporain de Vienne pourrait devenir s'il le peut le conservatoire improbable de l'inattendu, « le muséum de l'accident du temps réel. »

Le transfert de l'analogie à la numérologie qu'on appelle numérique me permet de rappeler que la numérologie était une religion. On passe de celle de la représentation, c'est-à-dire du recul, le souvenir, à la pure présentation. C'est le temps réel. Le réalisme, l'hyperréalisme du temps réel. L'hyperréalisme américain d'ailleurs a anticipé picturalement cette situation que j'appelais la télé-objectivité. L'hyperréalisme américain que Baudrillard a bien aimé a été introductif de l'hyper-réalité de l'accélération. L'instantanéité photographique a été la première machine de vision et la première machine de vitesse de l'instantanéité, bien plus que la fusée etc. Elle est initiale dans l'accélération de la réalité. Elle entraînera la naissance de la cinématographie. C'est-à-dire de la cinématique du défilement des images. Elle rendra visible les effets de la cinématique. On a oublié que la cinématique était l'énergie du visible. Il y a l'énergie cinétique, avec les accidents, les déplacements des corps avec les impacts. Mais, il y a aussi l'énergie cinématique. En ce sens, la chambre d'enregistrement de l'appareil est beaucoup plus importante que la machine de vitesse, la locomotive, qui va révolutionner le transport. Avec le cinéma, la photographie révolutionnera la transmission avec la télé et la télésurveillance en temps réel. Ainsi, à partir de la crise de l'instantanéité jusqu'à la télécommunication en direct, live, nous allons assister non plus seulement à l'accélération de l'histoire, mais à l'accélération de la réalité même. La présentation en temps réel des choses, des objets, des événements, va supplanter les anciennes représentations de l'espace réel. La présentation en temps réel va supplanter les représentations dans l'espace réel des œuvres picturales, sculpturales, ou architecturales, jusqu'à mettre en plastique de l'art contemporain qui, à partir de l'abstraction, va s'étendre à perte de vue en confondant les disciplines esthétiques de l'histoire. Ainsi à côté de l'objet et le sujet, la phase de la technologie, de l'objectivité, de la subjectivité va insérer ce qu'on pourrait dénommer sans erreur, la télé-objectivité et ses télé-subjectivités émotionnelles. Le tout, cette situation, vient de l'énergie du visible. C'est un mot auquel je tiens beaucoup, l'énergie du visible. Depuis la séquence filmique, la grande séquence, le photogramme, etc., jusqu'au vidéogramme télévisuel. Et tout ça, à côté de l'énergie cinétique des moyens de transport de notre modernité. Énergie cinétique des moyens du transport : le TGV, l'avion, la voiture, etc. L'énergie cinématique, personne ne reconnaît la cinématique comme énergie, l'énergie cinématique des transmissions. Transport, énergie cinétique. Transmission énergie cinématique, à la fois, audio et visuel.

En fait, comme l'économie politique, celle de la culture a subi deux coups de fouet : celui de l'accélération non seulement de l'histoire de l'art comme on dit au 19ème siècle, mais depuis peu, l'accélération de la réalité, grâce au progrès de la révolution d'information et des communications en temps réel qui bouleverse définitivement l'espace réel des formes, des arts plastiques au profit du temps réel et de la rythmologie (la rythmologie ici remplace la morphologie) de l'image et du son. C'est pour ça que je vous dis que l'art contemporain ou plutôt intemporain et sa morphologie ont subi l'assaut de la rythmologie quasiment musicale. Je répète que la musique est à l'origine de la vitesse. L'art contemporain et sa morphologie subissent l'assaut de la rythmologie quasi-musicale des performances et de diverses installations où se mêlent de plus en plus ce que l'on appelle le spectacle vivant.

On se trouve devant le deuil en lutte avec un art lumière, vitesse de la lumière, illumination, en route vers le devenir musical de l'image télévisée. Il faut choisir entre la dynamique et sa panique émotionnelle et, d'autre part, la mise en transe des foules subjuguées, c'est ça la musique, y compris la musique militaire. C'est ici et nulle part ailleurs que se joue désormais le sort de l'économie politique.

Wolfgang Schirmacher: J'ai besoin de mieux comprendre. Pourquoi devons-nous choisir? Pourquoi est-ce qu'on ne peut pas laisser les deux exister? Pourquoi est-ce qu'on ne peut pas dire: « aujourd'hui, mardi, c'est ma journée du corps et demain, mercredi, sera ma journée de l'esprit »?

Paul Virilio: Ça, c'est la liberté, quand il n'y a pas de choix, il n'y a pas de liberté. Moi, je suis architecte, n'oubliez jamais que je suis architecte et urbaniste et non pas philosophe. Je tiens aux formes, etc. Je termine en disant que le sort de l'économie politique, le sort du monde dépendent, non seulement de la politique de la richesse, mais de l'économie politique de la vitesse. Ça n'existe pas sauf chez les militaires avec la musique de marche. Le problème de l'économie politique de la démocratie est lié à l'économie politique de la vitesse. Aujourd'hui, on ne peut pas parler de tout ça sans l'écologie grise. C'est-à-dire l'écologie d'accélération de la réalité. Les futuristes avaient compris et les futuristes étaient quoi? Ils étaient fascistes. Je suis italien, j'admire Marinetti, mais pour moi ils ont introduit le fascisme. Je suis une victime de la blitzkrieg.

Question: Est-ce que ce n'est pas indissociable de voir la lumière et la matière ensemble en tant qu'architecte, est-ce que on ne voit pas le dynamique avec le statique?

Paul Virilio: L'architecture fournit la matière à une réception collective: instantanéité et simultanéité de la matérialité.

Question: La relation entre l'émotion et l'abstraction, et le côté transcendante qui est une lumière du pouvoir du divin. On a la transcendance et de l'autre côté l'immanence qui résiste à cette transcendance et s'oppose au pouvoir. Est-ce qu'on ne peut pas mettre tout ça en relation?

Paul Virilio: Je ne peux pas répondre à cette question parce que la situation est ouverte. Elle est *open*. Je ne maîtrise pas ce que je vous dis. Et je ne dis pas ça par modestie, mais par réalisme. On en a parlé depuis le début. Le travail que je fais est un travail d'approximation. Donc, on est dans la question essentielle, il faudrait un travail considérable pour répondre à cette question. Ceci dit, je peux même parler de la communauté d'intérêts de l'économie politique traditionnelle dans la démocratie et de la communauté d'émotions. On a là deux mondes qui sont radicalement différents. La communauté d'intérêts est liée à l'économie politique de la richesse, à l'état social, au socialisme, au communisme. De l'autre côté, le monde de la démocratie, la démocratie d'émotions, est lié à la vitesse des émotions. C'est-à-dire à l'inné. La première des émotions c'est la peur. C'est la puissance des émotions. C'est une émotion innée. Donc, on est devant une politique, une communauté d'émotions qui ne peut pas être démocratique. Si on arrive demain à standardiser les opinions comme ça été le cas avec les produits, on va standardiser les comportements. On ne peut pas standardiser les émotions sans les synchroniser. C'est-à-dire ce que tous pensent, la même émission au même moment : le temps réel. On est en dehors de la démocratie. On est dans une idéalité. On est devant un phénomène qui met fin à la démocratie. La démocratie de réflexe, n'est pas la démocratie de la réflexion. Le réflexe conditionné n'a rien à voir avec la réflexion en commun. C'est un gros travail qui sera fait dans l'université du désastre. C'est la mondialisation des affects en temps réel.

Question: Étant contre le fascisme et en faveur de la démocratie, je veux vous demander en tant qu'homme et sujet qui a des droits dans une démocratie, est-ce que l'art est un droit?

Paul Virilio: Oui

Continuation de question: Je veux parler du problème télévisuel. Depuis le début de la photographie, la matérialité de la photographie a laissé un résidu qu'on appelle l'archive. Par exemple en France, il y a des centaines de peintures, de dessins, de sculptures, répertoriés qui n'ont jamais été vu par le grand public. Que diriez-vous de l'idée d'utiliser la technologie pour pouvoir les distribuer au monde entier?

Paul Virilio: Je n'ai absolument rien contre la nouvelle technologie. Autrement dit, les gens disent, Virilio est technophobe. Non, je ne suis pas technophobe. Je suis même amateur de la nouvelle technologie. Depuis hier, j'essaie de vous dire que l'essentiel c'est la voie de la fin. La finitude et non pas la fin. La voie de finitude. On voit les archives. Quel est la finitude de l'archive? Si on ne parle pas de la finitude de l'archive à l'époque de la globalisation, on ne parle pas de l'archive. Quel est la finitude de l'archive? C'est la bibliothèque de Babel. Le livre de Borges. Donc, la question se pose aujourd'hui avec la bibliothèque de Babel, c'est-à-dire avec la possibilité de son échec dans son succès. On revient toujours à l'idée de la finitude que son succès est peut-être un échec. Que la plénitude peut devenir la finitude. Donc, il ne s'agit pas de nier l'importance de la bibliothèque de Babel. Il s'agit d'étudier aujourd'hui, à cause du temps réel, la globalisation dans sa finitude. A partir du moment où on aura étudié la finitude, c'est-à-dire l'accident, et en revenant à la tour de Babel, à la bibliothèque de Babel, on pourra parler de l'archive. Aujourd'hui on ne peut plus partir du commencement pour aller vers la fin. Il faut partir de la fin pour aller vers le commencement. La finitude du monde, de tout l'art est là. La finitude est devant nous, et il faut partir de la fin, non pas pour pleurer, « Oh, c'est affreux. » Non! Pour faire face à cette fin et pouvoir aller au-delà. Je ne sais pas où, d'ailleurs.

Question: Est-ce que vous dites que la dissémination globale de l'art digital continuera le processus d'aveuglement de la vision des spectateurs due à l'accélération et la surabondance qui peut mener à la finitude?

Paul Virilio: Je ne peux pas répondre parce que ça me dépasse. A partir du moment où on atteint la finitude de la globalité, on entre dans la mégalomanie ou la mégalopsychie. C'est pour ça que je dis que je ne peux pas le maîtriser. Ce n'est pas par modestie mais par réalisme. Personne, pas plus Einstein, Hawkins, Platon, ne peut maîtriser la globalisation. Je ne la maîtrise pas, et c'est un honneur. C'est ma force. C'est d'être un homme. Parce que face à ça je lis un livre d'un scientifique qui s'appelle Joël de Rosnay qui dirige la cité de la science à Paris qui est émerveillé par quoi? Le cerveau global. Le cerveau global qui serait la continuité de tous les cerveaux. Moi, je trouve que c'est une horreur. C'est le nom communiste pour l'intellectuel collectif. Je vous donne un exemple, après la guerre du Vietnam, j'avais un étudiant vietnamien qui est devenu professeur après et il a vécu la guerre du Vietnam contre les Américains. Il me disaitx: c'est extraordinaire, ça marchait très bien cet intellectualisme collectif, on faisait la guerre aux impérialistes. Chaque fois qu'on avait un problème, on envoyait un messager en vélo qui disait : voilà le problème. Ça peut être un problème de réduction d'eau, de réparations, etc. et les communistes dans 8 ou 10 jours, donnaient la réponse. L'intellectuel collectif vietnamien trouvait la réponse, youpi!

Question: Quand vous parlez de l'art sans pitié, j'ai l'impression que vous parlez d'une façon négative. Vous parlez d'un art qui a de la pitié. Ça me rappelle la critique de Nietzsche de la pitié, que l'objet de la pitié est gelé dans la forme de la pitié. Est-ce que vous voulez dire la pitié ou est-ce que vous pouvez également utiliser le mot empathie ou sympathie pour permettre le devenir de la pitié?

Paul Virilio: C'est une grande question et en même temps une petite question. On revient toujours à la même chose: les deux ordres de grandeurs de Bossuet. La grandeur de la puissance qui peut être impitoyable et la grandeur de la pauvreté qui est

pitoyable. Les deux sont liées. Le bien et le mal n'existe plus,
c'est génial! Je touche à cette question par l'espace-temps. Je
ne dis pas que c'est mauvais, c'est bon, mais par l'ampleur de
l'ordre de grandeur de puissance et de l'ordre de grandeur de
pauvreté de la faiblesse. Un monde qui dénie, comme ça été le
cas pendant la Deuxième Guerre mondiale, l'ordre de
grandeur de la pauvreté, de la faiblesse est un monde qui est
fini, qui s'épuise et qui mène à quoi? Au suicide global. Pas
seulement national, mais au suicide global. Le kamikaze est
d'une certaine façon le héros de ce monde impitoyable. Il est
même impitoyable vis-à-vis de lui-même. Ce n'est pas
seulement un suicide passif, je souffre, je ne peux plus, mais
un suicide actif: je veux que ma mort fasse mourir le monde.
On ne peut plus fonctionner avec cet ordre de grandeur de la
puissance. C'est ça la finitude. C'est ça la situation actuelle du
monde écologique.

C'est à partir de la fin et de la finitude qu'on peut reposer la
question de l'art, la question de l'empathie, la question des
mœurs, etc. Il y une situation qui nous dépasse, qui me
dépasse, parce que je suis inscrit dans l'ordre de la pitié, c'est-
à-dire la miséricorde. La miséricorde, la compassion est le
plus souvent considérée comme une faiblesse. Elle est une
puissance, celle de la faiblesse et on ne peut pas s'en
débarrasser sous peine de bercer dans le suicide collectif à la
japonaise, soit a l'américaine avec Hiroshima, etc. Je vous
donne un exemple de la grandeur de la pauvreté et de la
grandeur de puissance. Ce verre est d'une grandeur de
puissance absolue. Il est aussi grand qu'il peut être. Si ce verre
faisait trois milles mètres de haut, ça ne serait plus un verre.
Ce serait un château d'eau. La faiblesse, la pitié est une
puissance. Encore un exemple, j'ai assisté à une conférence et
il y avait un jeune historien du Moyen-Âge qui parlait du
pitoyable et de l'impitoyable. Au Moyen-Âge, les femmes, ont
employé des mots pour les chevaliers qui devenaient
« chevalier puce ». Autrement dit, il fait pitié. Pourquoi? Parce
que dans le rapport amoureux, il n'était pas impitoyable. Je
vous rappelle que le chevalier du Moyen-Âge est un arrache-
cœur. C'est vraiment le boucher, et pour elle, ce n'était pas

son chevalier, c'était de sa puce qu'elle avait pitié. C'est très fort. Le mot pitoyable n'est pas à sa place. Vous voyez? Le mot pitoyable ça veut dire, « ah » impitoyable, non, c'est l'inverse.

Question: Qui va financer l'université du désastre?

Paul Virilio: Je ne suis pas assez militant pour inaugurer l'université du désastre. Pas plus d'ailleurs pour inaugurer le musée du désastre. L'université du désastre c'est un livre. C'est ce que j'appelle une bouteille à la mer. Mes livres sont des bouteilles à la mer. On ouvre la bouteille, on lit le message et puis on le jette. Mes livres sont des bouteilles à la mer. Je n'ai aucune prétention à inaugurer cette université. Mais je sais qu'aujourd'hui, l'intellectuel n'est pas collectif, mais individuel. C'est quelque chose qui se substitue entre le spin-doctor, le directeur de la communication ou dans le domaine de services secrets, l'agent d'influence. Je suis donc un agent d'influence, rien de plus. Je ne suis payé ni par le KGB, ni par les Palestiniens, etc. Mais je considère que les intellectuels politiques comme dans le monde de Sartre, c'est fini quand un intellectuel a de l'influence. Qui a de l'influence? Seul le climat.

Question: Est-ce que l'accident peut-être la littérature? Je pense à la fugue et à la musique. Est-ce que l'accident peut aussi être artistique?

Paul Virilio: L'accident intégral concerne toutes les formes de la civilisation. L'accident est la suite de la poésie, suite du roman, suite de l'histoire, suite de la biologie, suite de l'astronomie. Bon, si cinquante mille ans sont nécessaires pour aller sur les autres planètes, c'est l'accident de l'astrophysique. Ça c'est l'accident intégral. Accident de toutes les disciplines. C'est pour ça qu'il y a l'universitaire. L'accident est universel et universitaire dans la finitude. C'est-à-dire dans la clôture du monde sur lui-même. C'est un événement qui nous dépasse infiniment, mais par contre on peut faire face ensemble à cela. Ensemble veut dire chacun à son tour. Bien sûr, c'est un événement, les accidents ont remplacé les événements. La rapidité du temps réel, l'accélération de la réalité, fait que des événements sont devenus les accidents par leur emplacement, par leur accélération même. Les événements sont de l'inattendu. D'une certaine façon, l'officier ancien attendait l'événement. On va vivre la guerre. Que tu l'attendes ou pas. Maintenant, on n'a même plus le temps d'attendre. Les choses arrivent sans qu'on s'y attende. L'accélération du temps est aussi l'accélération de l'événement. L'événement vient de l'accident. Les attentats étaient les attaques en image d'un événement accident. C'est un événement extraordinaire parce que ça remplace la guerre. Ce qui a déclenché la guerre du Pacifique. D'un côté, on a un événement qui a pris du temps, il s'est passé des choses entre Hirohito, le Président américain, etc. dans l'autre cas, paf! Il y a dix-huit jeunes hommes avec deux jets civils et ce n'est rien à côté des possibilités nucléaires, d'un accident concernant le monde, etc. Donc, l'accélération de la réalité, en accélérant tout événement, devient la question de l'histoire. Il y avait un anthropologue qui disait, « nous ne sommes plus que des anthropologues du présent. » Nous ne sommes plus des anthropologues de l'histoire de Charlemagne, etc., Nous sommes seulement des anthropologues du présent.

Question: L'art n'est plus un accident. On va vers une nouvelle génération d'artistes qui essayent de prévenir l'accident comme si l'art était présentatif. Et quand je parle de cela je parle surtout du jeu. En produisant l'art pour voir ce qui va se passer, on anticipe l'événement pour empêcher l'événement. Donc, je pense qu'on est suspendu. Je pense que l'art va vers l'accident et en faisant l'accident on trouvera plus de solutions pour beaucoup de questions qu'on se pose.

Paul Virilio: Deviner. Hier, comprendre était l'art des arts. Maintenant, il faut deviner. Deviner le bonheur, deviner le malheur. Deviner. Ce n'est pas l'avant-garde d'art, c'est l'attente de l'inattendu.

Wolfgang Schirmacher: L'idée c'est que dans le jeu, en faisant semblant d'embrasser l'accident, on empêche l'accident. Donc, le jeu est déjà un contrôle de l'accident.

Paul Virilio: La plupart des machines de simulation, je pense aux simulateurs militaires, aux simulateurs aéronautiques, c'est une simulation d'une conduite bizarre, c'est-à-dire que la simulation n'est pas une conduite normale. La conduite normale, on l'apprend aux commandes d'un avion. On apprend la conduite normale dans l'avion. Dans les simulateurs, on simule des catastrophes très bien, et l'heure du vol normal et l'heure du simulateur sont identiques.

Wolfgang Schirmacher: Mais, aujourd'hui l'artiste sait exactement ce qui est bien pour le marché, c'est l'accident. Mais, ils ne s'exposent pas vraiment eux-mêmes aux accidents. Ils simulent déjà ce contrôle.

Question: Est-ce qu'il y a peut être une façon de retenir la finitude à travers la mise-en scène ? En regardant Baudrillard par rapport à votre pensée, il dit que peut-être ça sera la réalité virtuelle qui sauve la réalité. Est-ce qu'on peut construire une représentation de la technologie plus humanisé et peut-être démilitariser les outils militaires?

Paul Virilio: La grande différence entre Jean et moi, c'est qu'il traitait de la simulation et moi de la substitution. Moi je choisis la substitution en disant qu'il y avait des époques du réel comme il y avait des époques de l'histoire et que la simulation qu'elle soit proverbe ou littéraire, littérale, la perspective annoncée par la renaissance, etc. laisse la place à un nouveau réel. C'est-à-dire la simulation homérique par exemple de la littérature de l'oralité passait dans la réalité. Les grands artistes de la littérature avaient simulé les situations magiques, mythiques qui devenaient totalement réelles et qui étaient banalisées. C'est pareil pour la voiture, c'est passé dans la réalité à notre époque. Aujourd'hui c'est pareil, la simulation informatique n'est pas moins importante que le grand *oratio* homérique ou les grandes fantaisies de Leonardo da Vinci. Donc, moi, ce qui m'intéresse c'est la phase de substitution. C'est le moment où la réalité change. Ce n'est pas le moment où elle est simulée par un art ou un autre. C'est le moment ou elle s'installe à sa place. Dans mon travail, on est dans la simulation, mais ce qui m'intéresse, c'est dans quelle substitution la réalité va-t-elle passer? Dans l'ordre de quelle réalité? Seulement pour moi, la simulation est une phase momentanée. L'important c'est quand la simulation devient réelle. Je vous donne un exemple au profit de la perspective. Pour moi, l'intention de la perspective, camera obscura, est un élément créé par l'histoire politique. La perspective est un phénomène politique, urbanistique et va tout modifier. Ce n'est pas par hasard si Machiavel, ce n'est pas par hasard si les villes de la Renaissance faisaient apparition, ce n'est pas par hasard l'économie politique de cette époque. Donc, la perspective de l'espace réel a été un moment extraordinaire. Je dis bien la perspective de la perception à travers la perception et non pas simplement du tableau, non, je vois en relief. Je voyais en relief sans savoir. Voir n'est pas savoir. Aujourd'hui si je fais une anticipation de la substitution de ce que vous venez dire, je pense que nous allons aller vers une vision perspective d'un temps réel, comment? Espace réel perspectivisme dans un sens, perspective du temps réel demain. La substitution est à venir. Quelle est cette perspective du temps réel? C'est ce que j'appelle la stéréo-réalité. Qu'est ce que la stéréo-réalité? C'est les graves et les aiguës et ça donne « Ping » un relief sonore, stéréophonique effet du champ grave, aiguë et je reçois le relief sonore. Stéréo-réel, stéréo-réalité, à ma disposition la vision actuelle, en actes, je vous vois, je suis avec vous dans l'espace réel, l'objet est devant moi et de l'autre coté, j'ai la vision actuelle virtuelle, une vision du champ qui me donne un autre relief de la perspective que celui de la renaissance italienne. Le relief stéréo-temporel, stéréo spatial. C'est pour ça que je ne suis pas contre les écrans, je ne suis pas technophobe. C'est un nouveau relief. Je voudrais raconter une petite anecdote à propos de Baudrillard et de la simulation et substitution. Quand on se retrouve à la revue *Travers*, je viens de signer ma campagne photographique qui m'a pris dix ans sur le Mur de l'Atlantique. Et Baudrillard a horreur des photos. Moi, je vais à la revue de *Travers*, parce qu'avant dans la revue *L'esprit*, il n'y avait pas de photos, pas d'images. Depuis longtemps, je ne fais plus des photos, mais lui, il en a fait. Il a même terminé en devenant photographe. C'est typique de notre mouvement.

Wolfgang Schirmacher: Un artiste aujourd'hui, un jeune artiste vous demande « Que devrais-je tenir de votre philosophie? Quel est votre conseil? » Vous n'avez pas de conseil, mais si vous aviez un conseil, ça serait quoi? Ma compréhension est que nous sommes dans un monde de la globalisation et celle de l'accélération par la vitesse. Ça, c'est notre situation, mais c'est une situation comme le destin auquel l'artiste ne peut que se joindre. En tant qu'artiste, vous pouvez y résister et trouver d'autres possibilités, comme les façons matérielles de faire les choses. Et tout ça c'est d'être conscient de ce qui se passe, de ne pas le nier, mais aussi de ne pas dire que c'est un fait, je dois m'y joindre.

Paul Virilio: Bon, je vais faire référence à un grand philosophe qui est aussi docteur de l'église, Augustin, St. Augustin qui avec Heidegger sont ceux qui parlait le mieux du temps: « Faites n'importe quoi, mais avec amour. » Piété, ayez pitié, pas forcément religieuse mais ayez pitié. Si vous le faites avec amour, avec pitié, vous pouvez le faire. Si tu le fais sans amour, sans pitié, ça devient impitoyable, ne fais pas. C'est ça la grandeur de la pauvreté. C'est ça l'amour philosophique, de la pitié philosophique, pas forcément un amour religieux. Si vous le faites par amour, vous pouvez le faire, sinon, arrêtez parce que de toute façon tout est foutu. Ce matin on a parlé de chevalier, du chevalier pitoyable, à propos de San Francisco et j'oublie quelqu'un, Don Quichotte: Le chevalier pitoyable, un des plus grands de la littérature.

Question: Je me demande, il y a bon nombre d'étudiants qui pensent qu'ils peuvent s'inscrire dans les écoles d'art et devenir artistes et le deviennent. D'après votre idée de l'accélération et de la proportion, on devient professeurs et admirateurs d'art, de plus en plus finis.

Paul Virilio: C'est le problème de la violence. La vitesse est la violence absolue. La vitesse est la violence des violences. Donc, quelque part le problème n'est pas de ralentir, c'est de prendre du recul pour mieux sauter. Reculer pour aller plus loin c'est-à-dire prendre de la distance. La distance focale, dans n'importe quel art, il faut trouver la focale. Il ne faut pas accepter le nez sur l'événement, il faut toujours reculer. Reculer comme dans la boxe pour allonger le poing. Reculer pour allonger. Ce n'est pas contre la violence, contre la vitesse. La vitesse est l'hypertrophie de la violence. Je prends cet exemple, si votre joue est à côté de la mienne, avec la même main, je peux caresser, je peux donner une gifle. Que fait la gifle? C'est le développent dans l'espace du poing, sinon c'est la caresse. Alors faites des caresses. Reprenez du recul. Il ne faut pas faire de la violence, ça ne sert à rien. Le grand enjeu d'aujourd'hui c'est le K non pas de Kafka mais du Kamikaze. J'ai parlé hier de la pollution de la distance. Vous vous souvenez, la pollution des substances: écologie verte. La pollution des distances, écologie grise. La distance, il faut la garder. D'où la nécessité de garder ce qu'on appelle l'allonge, jamais accepter d'être acculé comme les boxeurs dans les cordes. Quand on est acculé, on est foutu. Il faut toujours tourner comme dans la danse pour garder la distance. Toujours, c'est ça qui ne pollue pas la distance.

Question: Quelle est votre idée de l'éphémère? Ne pensez-vous pas que la dromologie appartienne à l'éphémère? Quel est la place dans la dromologie pour le fugitif?

Paul Virilio: C'est le contraire de Heidegger. « Toute grandeur est dans l'assaut. » Martin Heidegger. La fuite, c'est le recul. Je crois qu'aujourd'hui ce dont on a besoin c'est de recul, et le recul pour la victoire et non pas pour la fin. « Toute grandeur est dans l'assaut » c'est Stalingrad, c'est Verdun. La grandeur de la pauvreté, c'est reculer pour faire face. Comme je disais tout à l'heure d'un boxeur qui recule pour garder la distance.

Pour le kamikaze, toute grandeur est dans l'assaut, il arrive avec ses explosifs, et vous êtes tous morts. C'est Heidegger. Pour la puce, pour le pieux et le pitoyable, ce n'est pas comme ça. C'est dans le recul, dans la distance et dans l'intelligence. Il n'y a pas d'intelligence sans recul, sans représentation. C'est-à-dire sans se donner la focale de la raison. Dans l'attaque, l'individu est sans raison, il est déraisonnable. La fin du héros au sens traditionnel du terme. Le dernier héros, ce n'est pas Don Quichotte. C'est le kamikaze. Et moi, je dis que c'est Don Quichotte. Et vous aussi. Si vous êtes des artistes, vous ne pouvez pas être des kamikazes. C'est pour ça que je ne peux pas admettre l'activisme, ça préfigure le kamikaze. Celui qui met fin à sa vie et au monde. Alors, ça peut être un général qui appuie sur un bouton ou le pilote qui déclenche des bombes sur Hiroshima.

Question: Je crois qu'il y a un rapport avec la précarité.

Paul Virilio: Oui. Tout à fait. La grandeur de la pauvreté est la grandeur de la précarité. Si je ne suis rien, je suis tout. C'est le contraire de Marc Aurèle. « J'étais tout, empereur des romains, c'est rien.» Aujourd'hui c'est je ne suis rien et ce rien est tout: C'est le recul par rapport à l'orgueil du saut du chevalier. Siegfried ou Don Quichotte. Ça me rappelle un très bon livre de Milan Kundera qui s'appelle « Le Rideau ».

Cette façon de parler, de penser est ce qu'on appelle le contrecoup. C'est très intéressant. Quand on engloutit une fin, une finitude, l'histoire du monde engloutit la finitude de la géophysique. Quand on engloutit une fin, un mur, on recule, ça s'appelle le contrecoup. Il ne faut pas de contrecoup pour reculer. Par exemple quand on tire au fusil (j'étais soldat en Allemagne), ça fait mal surtout quand on a un 50-30. L'écologie est un recul. C'est la grandeur de pauvreté qui est un recul par rapport à la fin. Tout est contrefait dans a notion de finitude. Nous avons atteint la finitude, et donc, c'est par rapport à elle que nous pouvons penser, nous plaindre etc. Ce n'est pas triste.

Wolfgang Schirmacher: C'est exactement ce que dit Heidegger.

Paul Virilio: Ce n'est pas Heidegger. Ceci dit j'ai un grand respect pour Heidegger. L'histoire sur Heidegger et le nazisme, j'ai envie à dire au globe: un grand philosophe, un très grand peintre peut être aussi un monstre. Et oui, le Caravage par exemple, grand peintre et assassin. On peut être un grand philosophe et politiquement un monstre. Je ne dis pas que Heidegger était un monstre, mais puisqu'il a été à Freiburg, ça ne signifie pas, pour autant qu'il n'était pas un grand philosophe. Quand je disais le Caravage, les gens disent quelle horreur, des assassins, mais ses beaux tableaux n'ont rien de monstrueux.

Question: J'ai une question à propos du transfert de la représentation à la présentation. Il me parait que ça ressemble à la variation du dessin chez Aristote entre le mimésis et la diogénisa. Donc, ma question est: la dromologie fonctionne-t-elle comme une sorte de théâtre?

Paul Virilio: Bien sûr la dromologie participe déjà dans la mise en scène du monde. Elle a remplacé la transparence de l'espace des choses, la transparence de l'eau, de l'air, le verre par la trans-apparence du temps. La télé-perception est une trans-apparence du temps réel alors que le verre est une trans-apparence du verre. Et c'est la notion de transparence qui a évolué par l'accélération de la réalité. Dans la réalité, quand l'espace réel domine sur le temps de l'instantanéité, la transparence était d'un matériau, le verre, l'eau, l'air, avec le brouillard etc. Avec la portance du temps réel, on monte dans la trans-apparence. C'est-à-dire une apparence instantanément transmise à distance par la vertu du temps réel. C'est la vertu de l'espace réel de l'atmosphère, l'autre c'est la trans-apparence de la transmission. La vitesse participe à cette mise en forme de la trans-apparence. C'est pour ça que je parle au niveau politique du trans-politique. Nous sommes au niveau de la tyrannie du temps réel c'est-à-dire de l'accélération de la

réalité. Nous sommes dans la trans-politique. Trans-apparence,
c'est la vitesse de la lumière.

*Question: Avec l'accélération de la transmission, pouvez-vous
parlez de la réplication des images?*

Paul Virilio: Le texte introductif de Walter Benjamin, *L'image
d'art et sa reproduction*, a pris des proportions considérables
avec le clonage. Le grand danger de l'uniformisation du
monde, c'est le clonage, non seulement des images mais des
êtres à travers la génétique. C'est le conformisme intégral.
C'est-à-dire qu'on entre dans la logique de la célérité où tout
est redoublé à l' infini comme dans un miroir qui redouble les
images. Donc, le conformisme de la modernité est bien pire
que l'académisme avec les standards et les looks des styles,
des genres, des modes qui règnent pendant un certain
temps. C'est la possibilité d'un modèle unique, pas
simplement ce qu'on a appelé le politiquement correct, mais
l'optiquement correct. Il y a rien de pire que d'imaginer
l'optiquement correct. *Optical correct* OK. C'est ça qui nous
menace avec les possibilités de reproduction non seulement
des images, mais des standards de situation avec la
synchronisation. D'où je dirais l'échec du succès. Pour moi
aujourd'hui la célébrité est morte réellement. Je ne le dis pas
par modestie parce que je suis un phénomène, non. Je dis
aujourd'hui que quelqu'un qui est célèbre dans son système de
conformisme ne présente aucun intérêt. Zidane est un très bon
joueur de football, rien à redire. Shakespeare était un grand
auteur et philosophe. Shakespeare est célèbre, pourquoi? Il
participe à une célébration transhistorique. Zidane ne sert à
rien. D'une certaine façon, la célébrité est morte au profit de la
célébration. Avant la célébrité, c'était un individu, un malin
qui d'un coup faisait la différence dans n'importe quel
domaine. Aujourd'hui c'est la célébration d'un standard, que
ce standard soit une star médiatique comme Madonna ou
comme un grand philosophe, Bernard Henri-Lévy, etc. pour
moi c'est fini, terminé. La célébrité est morte dans ce
conformisme médiatique. Je vous donne un exemple. Henri
Michaux, je peux en citer d'autres, ça n'a pas d'importance,

Michaux, pas d'interview, rien, pas de photo, jamais, silence.
Il existe par le silence et le retrait par rapport à l'illumination
trans-apparence. On le voit avec Pynchon, un grand écrivain
contemporain. Je vais vous raconter une petite anecdote d'un
grand dessinateur français, Forain. Forain était un dessinateur
humoristique. Forain était invité à une grande exposition de
peintres et de dessinateurs du XIX° siècle. Il arrive, il regarde
les dessins. Il contemple...il contemple et il puis il s'en va. Un
artiste le voit et dit « Monsieur Forain, monsieur Forain!» et
puis il voit la tête de Forain qui n'est pas très emballé par ce
qu'il avait vu et à ce moment il dit: « il faut bien vivre ».
Forain lui rétorque : « pour faire ce que tu fais, je n'en vois pas
l'intérêt ». C'est très intéressant. C'est très important, c'est
qu'il ne critiquait pas. Il sentait qu'il n'avait pas apprécié et
qu'il n'avait rien à dire et il n'a rien dit. L'autre vient et dit
« Il faut bien vivre ». Ce n'est pas un moyen de vivre, c'est un
moyen de survivre. La question n'est pas d'aimer les dessins,
c'est que le peintre a justifié ses dessins par le besoin de vivre.
Je vous donne encore un exemple. Quand j'étais très jeune,
pratiquement aucun des amis ne vivait de ses peintures, de son
œuvre. Tous avaient un double métier. Je ne citerai personne,
je connais des architectes du monde entier. Je suis très inquiet
maintenant par beaucoup d'entre eux qui ont beaucoup de
talent parce qu'ils ont développé la grandeur de la puissance.
Ils ont développé leurs agences avec 150 dessinateurs. C'est
colossal. Le résultat: Pour garder leur agence, ils sont obligés
de faire un peu n'importe quoi. Et petit à petit, ils perdent du
terrain. Et ils n'ont jamais été aussi connus que maintenant.

*Question: Pouvez-vous parler de la question de la séparation
et de la projection de l'identité en ligne?*

Paul Virilio: A mon avis, c'est une illusion de la liberté.
L'homme et la femme sont uniques comme les empreintes
digitales. On le sait, avec l'ADN et l'empreinte digitale. Les
technologies vont non seulement permettre le clonage de
l'identique, mais aussi la technification de la différence. Je
viens d'une famille, une tribu, au sein de laquelle je suis un
individu. A mon avis, c'est la diaspora de la liberté. La

dispersion de la liberté. Alors, au niveau du théâtre, c'est pleinement reconnu. C'est propre au théâtre : l'acteur et son double. Au niveau du théâtre social, à mon avis on entre dans une dramaturgie qui conduit à la perte de l'identité. Il y a un acquis, mais il n'y a pas d'acquis sans perte. Pouvoir être plusieurs personnes à la fois, c'est un acquis, mais avec le risque de se perdre. Il y a une phrase du Christ dans les Évangiles, « A quoi sert de balayer le monde si on se perd? »

Cela ne veut pas dire qu'il ne faut pas jouer, qu'il ne faut pas avoir votre avatar, etc. évidemment, ce n'est pas interdit. Ça veut dire qu'il faut poser la question jusqu'à sa limite. C'est toujours la même question: jusqu'au bord de quoi? La limite du jeu de rôle, c'est quoi? Si on ne pose pas la question de la limite, à mon avis, on ne peut pas jouer. Si on ne pose pas la question de la limite, je trouve qu'on devient dépersonnalisé.

Question: Pouvez-vous parler de votre lien avec Max Stirner?

Paul Virilio: Je faisais partie des gens qui ont été intéressés par l'anarchie. Quand on est un petit peu libre, on s'intéresse à l'anarchie surtout quand on est jeune. Et donc, la question de « l'unicité de l'être » est donc une question tellement évidente qu'on est obligé de la justifier. Aujourd'hui on voit à quel point on est déjà désorganisé, en décomposition. En '68 j'ai fait partie des gens qui se sont agités au théâtre de l'Odéon dans ce mouvement, la premier phrase que j'ai lancée sur la scène de l'Odéon, « on ne compose pas avec une société en décomposition. » Autrement dit j'étais déjà sensible à l'anarchie, elle est dé-compositrice.

En mai '68 il y avait deux lieux, la Sorbonne pour les communistes, et le théâtre de l'Odéon pour les anarchistes et les situationnistes. Par exemple, je me souviens d'un des grands amphis au moment de '68, quelqu'un avec un gant d'une couleur très précise montait dans le plus grand amphi de la Sorbonne en disant « Je viens de lire sur les murs que l'imagination prend le pouvoir. C'est faux, c'est le peuple qui a pris le pouvoir. » Et moi j'ai hurlé, « Alors, c'est que tu dénies l'imagination au peuple. » C'était un truc de jeunesse.

Question: J'essaie de mettre ensemble ce que vous avez dit ce matin et cet après-midi sur l'art et la politique. Vous avez décrit une situation où on déplace le régime de la représentation et quelque chose d'autre prend sa place. Je ne pense pas seulement que c'est nécessairement la présentation parce que ça c'est un retour du passé, mais peut-être c'est le rythme du processus de la présentation en temps réel, la synchronisation et la globalisation du temps réel. Et je vois tout ça comme une sorte de résonance. Peut-être on part du régime de la présentation pour arriver à celui de la résonance.

Paul Virilio: Oui, bien sûr, mais là on est obligé de faire des oppositions représentation/présentation, espace réel du temps d'un côté et espace du temps réel de l'autre côté. Evidemment, c'est l'effet accidentel qui change tout, le mot-clef, etc. Il s'agit de ne pas être évacué. Le propre du temps réel, c'est sa puissance de dominer. Ce n'est pas le temps réel qui est dangereux, c'est à partir du moment où il devient le temps unique de la présentation la plus importante. Tout le reste est discriminé. Le danger n'est pas la vitesse et la violence absolue. Le problème, ce n'est pas la vitesse, c'est que ça devienne de plus en plus soutenu et que la présentation « live », directe, l'instantanéité dominent définitivement le temps de la représentation.

On sait bien qu'il y a substitution. On le voit bien à ce moment. Je prends un exemple, quand on crée un objet technique, on en élimine un autre. Par exemple, il n'y plus de machine à écrire. Moi, je tape, c'est ma femme qui tape, en fait, je ne suis pas doué pour ça. Il n'y a plus de machine à écrire, il n'y a que des ordinateurs. Moi, je suis désolé, mais il y a encore des chevaux. La grande question aujourd'hui, c'est que demain, il n'y aura plus de chevaux et plus que des voitures. C'est demain, il n'y a plus de traitements de texte et plus jamais de stylos. Le problème c'est la dominance. Le problème est que la science est économe.

Elle découvre, comme on découvre un continent. Ensuite, elle exploite, et enfin, elle s'en va. Cette dimension exploitante de la science, ça existe aussi dans les technologies. Ce que je crains, ce n'est pas la présentation et sa résonance de la représentation. Ça fait partie de la musicalité: cette puissance de conditionnement, de la vitesse absolue de la lumière, éliminerait le mouvement. Je prends un exemple, dans la transmission du transport, quand on descend de sa voiture, on n'est pas obligé de sortir d'un côté ou d'un autre, vous êtes d'accord? On peut marcher. Mais si on continue comme ça, on ne pourra plus marcher. C'est vrai dans l'ordre de la technologie, vous voyez ce que je veux dire? Le moyen de transport que sont mes jambes est pris en compte par la voiture qui me transporte, mais je peux le mettre au garage et aller me promener. De même, monter à cheval c'est vachement agréable etc. Le danger c'est qu'un jour, on ne puisse plus marcher, parce qu'il y a un tapis roulant, parce qu'il y aurait un engin spécial qui relie ma motricité, etc. Il ne faut pas oublier cette possibilité d'élimination du progrès: le progrès éliminatoire. Si le progrès n'est pas éliminatoire, il n'y a aucun problème, c'est un plus. Les gens me disent « comment tu écris à la machine à écrire, ça ne va pas non? » De quel droit ? Je t'emmerde, moi. J'aime ma machine à écrire. Je dis, qui a interdit la machine à écrire? Qui a interdit d'écrire au stylo? J'envoie des lettres au stylo, des manuscrits, je rappelle qu'il y a des vendeurs d'autographes, que Hugo a écrit des lettres à la main qui sont vendues pour des centaines de dollars, mais quand j'envoie une lettre à quelqu'un écrite à la main, il me dit: « Quand même, tu n'as pas de respect pour moi? » A bon, vous voulez que je vous tape une lettre avec la machine? Vous vous rendez compte du discrédit? C'est selon moi, l'élimination du progrès.

Dans mon école où j'enseignais, j'ai lancé un laboratoire d'informatique. Ça marchait tellement bien que même les métros parisiens envoyaient leurs ouvriers dans notre atelier d'informatique leurs ouvriers. Et les voitures. J'ai une magnifique Jaguar. C'est rapide. Je l'aime bien comme ça. Le dynamisme de la technique.

Question: Je me demande si je comprends la différence entre l'art intemporain et l'art contemporain.

Paul Virilio: Il y a une citation très bien dans mon livre sur l'art, le dialogue d'Auguste Rodin et Paul Roussel où Rodin fait allusion à l'homme qui marche. Et il s'est posé la question sur la mobilité du corps. Il s'intéressait comme Giacometti à un moment important. Et Paul Roussel défend la photo de l'instantané, en disant « Non, ton bonhomme est ridicule, tu vois comment il marche. » Et Rodin dit, « non, parce que dans la réalité, le temps ne s'arrête pas. En moi, dans mes sculptures, j'ai tenu compte du temps qui dure. C'est pour ça que j'ai modifié la position. » En regardant ce personnage, on voit le temps qui passe, le temps de la marche. Pas simplement comme la photo instantanée. C'est pareil dans les tableaux de Degas quand il fait les chevaux de course.

Les pattes des chevaux ne correspondaient pas à la réalité du tout. C'est très compliqué de voir les pieds des chevaux. Et il a fallu Muybridge pour voir comment mettre les positions des pattes de chevaux. Il y a là un grand débat sur le temps qui passe et le temps qui s'arrête. Le temps réel de l'instantanéité est un temps arrêté. Non pas arrêté au sens de la fixité. Mais arrêté au sens de l'écoulement du temps. C'est complexe, et en même temps, c'est très évident. Pour quelqu'un qui a fait de la sculpture, de la peinture, comme Degas, on comprend bien ça. Je voudrais bien distinguer l'intemporel et l'intemporain. L'intemporel c'est ce qui arrête le temps, c'est l'instantanéité et j'ai dit que l'art intemporel arrête la filiation aux arts anciens depuis la renaissance, le classicisme, etc. Toute l'histoire de l'art, l'histoire de la peinture et de la sculpture n'est qu'un long travelling où les différentes phases de l'histoire de l'art s'enchaînent. A partir du 19ème siècle, avec la révolution industrielle, l'art moderne est coupé de ses filiations. L'art intemporain, c'était cet art de la coupure avec les filiations. C'est un art désaffilié. Ce néologisme, l'intemporain, est important parce que ça traduit bien l'accident du temps. C'est le temps qui a été accidenté par la parution de l'instantanéité. Quelque part le mot intemporain montre qu'on ne peut pas être contemporain parce qu'on s'inscrit dans l'histoire moderne.

Question: Est-ce que la photo est devenue le péché originel?

Paul Virilio: La première machine de vision qui a tout lancé, c'est l'appareil photo. On ne peut pas comprendre la télésurveillance généralisée sans l'appareil photo. Par exemple, il y a en ce moment trois millions de caméras de surveillance à Londres. N'importe quelle personne qui se balade à Londres est filmée trois cent fois par jour. Tout ça est sorti du « click, clac, kodak. »

Le progrès de la vitesse est aussi le progrès de l'élimination. La vitesse est liée à la course. La course est le progrès de l'élimination. Le (con) cours...c'est un jeu de mots. C'est l'élimination. Le concours, c'est compétition, élimination. C'est la grandeur de la pauvreté.

Question: Nous savons que l'histoire est pour les vainqueurs, tu parles de la grandeur de la pauvreté qui est essentielle. Quels sont les moyens que nous avons devant nous pour la mettre en valeur?

Paul Virilio: Nous avons les moyens devant nous. C'est-à-dire pour la dernière élimination, la biosphère, on retrouve l'écologie grise. Ce qui est éliminé par la vitesse, c'est la terre. C'est-à-dire l'environnement. Au profit d'une recherche d'exo-planètes. D'une planète exotique, d'un ailleurs. Quand on dit externalisation, éliminer, ce n'est pas simplement l'élimination des chevaux par rapport aux voitures, la machine à écrire par l'ordinateur, c'est que la terre est trop petite pour supporter la vitesse. La terre est réduite à rien, autrement dit à la grandeur de la pauvreté par l'accélération provoquée. D'où la revendication des grands scientifiques: « Il faut aller ailleurs ».

Si on veut survivre, selon Stephen Hawking, il faut absolument trouver une autre planète. C'est de la folie. C'est de la philo-folie. On est dans un monde de la folie. La science est devenue la science opératoire, pas celle du savoir, celle de la connaissance. Ce qu'on appelle la techno-science est une farce par son succès d'éliminer la terre. Non seulement par la pollution dans l'écologie, mais aussi par la pollution des distances et du temps. C'est-à-dire la grandeur nature. La grandeur nature est devenue la petitesse dans le monde et c'est impensable. Celui qui dit ça est un fou. Pas un fou dans le sens des aliénés dont parlait Foucault et autres, mais au sens de la philosophie, au sens de la sagesse. Ces derniers darwinistes qui disent: « Eliminez les plus faibles, c'est la terre qui est devenue trop faible pour le progrès. Trop petite, trop ridicule. Trop paumée. Il nous faut une autre terre! » C'est la pure folie! C'est la mégalopsychie et pas la mégalomanie.

Je pense en particulier aux élections quand Nicolas Hulot dit qu'il faut absolument une rencontre sur le réchauffement climatique et le problème de pollution etc. Les scientifiques, les astrophysiciens nous disent qu'il faut trouver une planète exotique. Ça ne marche pas, ou c'est l'un ou c'est l'autre. Il y a une contradiction absolue. La science ne peut pas chercher une autre planète à coloniser et au même moment sauver la planète. Il y a une contradiction absolue. La grande science de l'astronomie, qui s'est intéressée à la terre, nous dit : Attention la terre est polluée, il faut la préserver. Puis dans le même moment elle nous dit : « Mais on peut trouver peut-être en fin de compte une planète dans le système solaire dans cinquante mille ans pour le voyage. Là, il y a une folie, on ne peut pas parler de l'écologie et en même temps des exo-planètes. C'est ici et maintenant!

Question: Je suis intéressé à ce que vous avez dit tout à l'heure à propos de l'amour comment l'artiste devrait se positionner. Je pense à la question du cadeau: donner le cadeau sans rien attendre. Donc, ma question est : est-ce que l'amour est un accident?

Paul Virilio: Sûrement pas.

Question: Justement l'amour n'est pas un accident, mais est-ce qu'on ne peut pas regarder l'art comme l'amour? Est-ce qu'il y a un mouvement de l'art comme un art « inaccidenté »?

Paul Virilio: Oui, il n'y a pas de substance sans accident. L'accident et la substance sont l'envers et le revers de la même médaille. Hannah Arendt dit que le progrès et la catastrophe sont l'envers et le revers de la même médaille. Je vous donne un exemple, Airbus, 800 places, 800 morts. Donc, il n'y a pas de substance, il n'y a pas de distance sans accident.

Question: Je voudrais que vous parliez de la notion de l'absence qui est présente avec l'accident. C'est comme le non-être.

Paul Virilio: Non, c'est comme un sommeil de la conscience. Nous sommes éveillés dans la mesure où nous dormons. Nous sommes vivants dans la mesure où nous sommes mortels. Ceux qui disent « je ne veux pas mourir », ne peuvent pas être vivants. L'éveil, il faudrait parler de la coupure de sommeil, je n'en suis pas capable, il faut parler de Freud et de la notion de sommeil paradoxal, etc. Le sommeil est un monde à part. Même la nuit et le jour, on est devant la logique de l'être qui est visuel et obscur: L'éveil c'est la présence et l'absence.

Mon seul professeur de morale c'est un chat. J'avais huit ou dix ans. J'étais à Nantes, avant les bombardements. On est dans la rue et il y avait un chat qui appartenait à un marchand. J'aimais bien ce chat et le chat m'aimait bien. C'est important d'avoir un animal domestique à la maison. Moi, j'aimais ce chat, je le caressais. Et il se laissait toujours faire. Et j'aimais tellement ce chat que j'ai décidé de le caresser tout le temps et il m'a griffé. Il avait raison. Il en a eu marre. C'est ça la morale. Ce pauvre chat, ce n'est pas la privation, « trop c'est trop.» Il fallait faire une coupure. Il fallait caresser et après, le laisser. La coupure...

Contributors

Paul Virilio is a renowned urbanist, political theorist and critic of the art of technology. Born in Paris in 1932, Virilio is best known for his 'war model' of the growth of the modern city and the evolution of human society. He is also the inventor of the term 'dromology' or the logic of speed. Identified with the phenomenology of Merleau-Ponty, the futurism of Marinetti and technoscientific writings of Einstein, Virilio's intellectual outlook can usefully be compared to contemporary architects, philosophers and cultural critics such as Bernard Tschumi, Gilles Deleuze and Jean Baudrillard. Virilio is the author, among other books of *Speed and Politics, The Information Bomb, Open Sky,* and most recently, *The Original Accident.* He is currently professor of Urban Philosophy at the European Graduate School, Saas-Fee, Switzerland.

Hubertus von Amelunxen is the Walter Benjamin Chair at European Graduate School and founding professor of several institutions and Schools. He is the author of books on photography and media and has curated many international exhibitions, most recently together with Dieter Appelt and Peter Weibel "Notation. Calculus and Form in the Arts" (2008/2009)

Drew Burk studied philosophy, religion and political anthropology at L'Institut D'Etudes Politiques in Aix-en-Provence. He has translated work by Jean Baudrillard, Jacques Derrida, and Paul Virilio. He is a doctoral student in Media and Communications at the European Graduate School.

Jason Adams is a PhD Candidate in Media and Communication at the European Graduate School and in Political Science at the University of Hawai'i. He is currently writing *The Sense of Belonging*, a genealogy of the modern citizen-subject as constructed through the postwar American sensory-memory habitus of sight, sound and smell.

Sean Smith is a critical sport theorist and artist living in Toronto. He publishes a blog titled *sportsBabel*, which examines the aesthetics, politics and poetics of the sportocracy at the intersections between the material and immaterial. *www.sportsbabel.net*

Michael Hirsch is a graduate of both the University of Chicago (AB '98, English Language and Literature) and the Yale University Divinity School (M.Div. '03). Professionally, he has worked in healthcare chaplaincy and global mental health. He is currently a doctoral candidate at the European Graduate School. His current research interests involve political theology, philosophy of science and international public health.

Daniel Brittain studied Philosophy, Literary Theory, and Theatre Studies at Evergreen State College. A perverse librarian who does not have a drivers license, he is fascinated by the relationship between speed and expenditure in the creation of ontic-moments. He enjoys playing games imagining constraints of being from the pre-historic onward. Daniel currently resides in Olympia, Washington.

Jon Thrower graduated with a MA in English from Southeast Missouri State University. He is an author of *Balancing on a Bootheel* an anthology of young Missouri poets. He currently teaches at colleges in the St. Louis area. His interests are writing pedagogy, creative writing, critical theory, mixology, and eclectic voice phenomenology. He has an 'A' in the school of life.

—— *books available from Atropos Press*

Teletheory. Gregory L. Ulmer

Philosophy of Culture-Kulturphilosophie: Schopenhauer and Tradition. Edited by Wolfgang Schirmacher.

Grey Ecology. Paul Virilio
Edited with introduction by Hubertus von Amelunxen. Translated by Drew Burk

Laughter. Henri Bergson. Translated by Drew Burk

Talking Cheddo: Liberating PanAfrikanism. Menkowra Manga Clem Marshall

The Tupperware Blitzkrieg. Anthony Metivier

Che Guevara and the Economic Debate in Cuba. Luiz Bernardo Pericás

Follow Us or Die. Vincent W.J. van Gerven Oei and Jonas Staal

Just Living: Philosophy in Artificial Life. Collected Works Volume 1.
Wolfgang Schirmacher

Think Media: EGS Media Philosophy Series

Wolfgang Schirmacher, editor

The Ethics of Uncertainty: Aporetic Openings. Michael Anker

Trans/actions: Art, Film and Death. Bruce Alistair Barber

Trauma, Hysteria, Philosophy. Hannes Charen and Sarah Kamens

Literature as Pure Mediality: Kafka and the Scene of Writing.
Paul DeNicola

Deleuze and the Sign. Christopher M. Drohan

The Suicide Bomber and Her Gift of Death. Jeremy Fernando

Hospitality in the age of media representation. Christian Hänggi

Transience: a poiesis, of dis/appearance. Julia Hölzl

**The Organic Organisation: freedom, creativity and
the search for fulfilment.** Nicholas Ind

Media Courage: impossible pedagogy in an artificial community.
Fred Isseks

Mirrors triptych technology: Remediation and Translation Figures.
Diana Silberman Keller

Sonic Soma: Sound, Body and the Origins of the Alphabet. Elise Kermani

The Art of the Transpersonal Self: Transformation as Aesthetic and Energetic Practice.
Norbert Koppensteiner

Can Computers Create Art? James Morris

Propaganda of the Dead: Terrorism and Revolution. Mark Reilly.

The Novel Imagery: Aesthetic Response as Feral Laboratory. Dawan Stanford.

Community without Identity: The Ontology and Politics of Heidegger. Tony See